Praise for *The Pig an*

"Baby-boom trends are the key to creating wealth. This fascinating book tells you how."

—*Harry Dent Jr., author of* The Great Boom Ahead *and the forthcoming* The Roaring 2000s

"This is one of the best-researched books on demographics I have ever read!"

—*Elaine Garzarelli, Ph.D., President, Garzarelli Capital, Inc.*

"Want an enjoyable, easy-to-read course in modern economics? And learn how to invest in the most profitable trends? This is your book. You will finally understand the kind of forces that drive the world economy. I highly recommend *The Pig and the Python.*"

—*Sam Case, registered investment adviser and author of* The First Book of Investing

"An illuminating tale of a boomer couple preparing for a secure future."

—*David Chilton, author of* The Wealthy Barber: Everyone's Guide to Becoming Financially Independent

"*The Pig and the Python* charmingly guides the reader along a lively path to understanding how the demographic impact of the largest population of this century—the baby boomers—affects consumption trends, business trends, and stock market selection and cycles. The authors shed light on how to easily incorporate this knowledge into prudent investment planning. A delight!"

—*Louise Yamada, Senior Technical Analyst, VP Research, Smith Barney, and author of the forthcoming book* Market Magic

"With so many boomers caught in a state of 'financial paralysis,' this book provides an illuminating and much needed perspective on ways in which boomers can prepare for their financial future."

—*Ken Dychtwald, Ph.D., President and CEO, Age Wave, LLC*

"David Cork's book captures the economic tsunami created by the demographics of the baby boom generation . . . investors should take note!"

—*Dan Jaworski, BPI Global Asset Management*

"A timely and engaging analysis of the impact of changing demographics on personal investment planning."

—*Dr. David K. Foot, author of the bestselling* Boom, Bust & Echo

"Demographics, like geological change, is so slow that most of the time we don't notice it happening until we look back and notice that the world, not so long ago, used to be a very different place. As the first human society ever dominated numerically by the elderly, our psychology, sociology, government, and businesses are all about to be different. *The Pig and the Python* is a good place to start if one wants to look forward and understand what is about to happen."

—*Lester C. Thurow, Professor of Economics, former Dean of Sloan School of Management, Massachusetts Institute of Technology (MIT)*

The
Pig
and
the
Python

HOW TO
PROSPER
FROM THE
AGING
BABY BOOM

DAVID CORK
WITH SUSAN LIGHTSTONE

PRIMA PUBLISHING

The authors are grateful to:
Greg Keelor of Blue Rodeo for permission to quote lines from "The Ballad of the Dime Store Greaser and the Blonde Mona Lisa," by Greg Keelor.
Daniel Stoffman for permission to quote from his work.
Michael Smythe, president and CEO of Proof in Advance Education Corp. of Toronto, for permission to use his Internet idea, "BoomerBytes."
Dan Richards, president, Marketing Solutions, for the use of his phrase "GIC refugees."

Library of Congress Cataloging-in-Publication Data

Cork, David.
The pig and the python: how to prosper from the aging baby boom / by David Cork and Susan Lightstone.
p. cm.
Originally published: Toronto: Stoddart, 1996.
Includes bibliographical references.
ISBN 0-7615-1275-6
1. Finance, Personal. 2. Baby boom generation. I. Lightstone, Susan. II. Title.
HG179.C6833 1997
332.024'00971—dc21   97-37319
                                                               CIP

98 99 00 01 02 HH 10 9 8 7 6 5 4 3 2 1
Printed in the United States of America

Although the author has exhaustively researched all sources to ensure the accuracy and completeness of the information contained in this book, we assume no responsibility for errors, inaccuracies, omissions, or any other inconsistency herein. Any slights of people or organizations are unintentional. Readers should use their own judgment and/or consult a financial expert for specific applications to their individual situations.

How to Order
Single copies may be ordered from Prima Publishing, P.O. Box 1260BK, Rocklin, CA 95677; telephone (916) 632-4400. Quantity discounts are also available. On your letterhead, include information concerning the intended use of the books and the number of books you wish to purchase.

Visit us online at www.primapublishing.com

Contents

If I am of any use
to this old world,
I am so because of you.

To our mothers,
Joan and Doreen

Acknowledgments

Two books—*The Great Boom Ahead* by Harry Dent Jr. and *Age Wave* by Ken Dychtwald—have had an enormous influence on me, both professionally and personally. Both books concern demographics and the ways the baby boom influences just about every aspect of our lives. It became obvious to me that this generation would eventually hit—and hit hard—the financial markets. Over the past several years the financial advice I provide to my clients has become increasingly influenced by demographics. Not only does the study of demographics cast light on the study of economics, it also provides a better way to understand the pressures that our population brings to bear on the financial and commodity markets.

Given that the study of demographics is . . . well . . . so human, I decided to humanize my ideas, putting them into a framework of a story—a tale about boomers. Susan Lightstone and I have created fictional characters, but the demographic and financial facts they discuss are real—facts that I use in my seminars on the impact of the boom on investing. In those seminars I explain the "why" of investing in the stock markets, telling audiences how the baby boom is making the market a very attractive place to be. This theme forms the cornerstone of our book.

There are many people we would like to thank who have aided us in our work. David Chilton offered his wisdom and friendship at every stage of the writing process. I am grateful for his guidance. Ben Dominitz, Prima's publisher, provided enthusiasm accompanied by sage advice. Michael Smythe, my best friend, has acted as my ideas adviser for many years. His good sense is reflected in these pages. Thanks, Mike.

I have been privileged to work with demographic experts, the members of the Madison Avenue Demographics Group. Tom McCormack, Rick Loreto, and David Foot have enriched my work and I am deeply indebted to them. Allan Shaw and Louise Yamada of Smith Barney in New York generously shared their ideas and technical work concerning demographics. Meddi Shaw, an investment adviser with Smith Barney in New York, and Jeffrey Harris, a tax and investment adviser in Harrisonburg, Virginia, offered helpful insights on the financial aspects of the book. I would also like to thank David Speck of O'Donnell Investment Management for his kind assistance.

Many people spent time and energy reading and discussing the contents of this book with us. Rachel Leaney, always cheerful and clever, patiently answered our many, many requests for information. Jason Brazeau, assistant extraordinaire, not only delivered excellent work but also his views on the mindset of the baby-bust generation. Bill Kretzel and Anne Willison offered intelligent insights and keen research skills.

ACKNOWLEDGMENTS

Thanks to Stuart McCormack, our lawyer, and Debra Venzke and Paula Munier Lee, our editors at Prima, who handled our work with thoroughness and accuracy. Daphne King at Spectrum United Mutual Funds was a font of information, especially concerning Generation X and the usefulness of station wagons. Thank you to Jim O'Reilly and Marilyn A. Moran of the Greater Boston Real Estate Board for the time they spent discussing our ideas. We are grateful to the librarians at the State Library of Massachusetts for their help. In particular, I would like to thank Sheila Martel for sharing her views on the collective soul of our generation. She may be the wisest person I have ever met. A special thank you to media consultants Barry McLoughlin and Laura Peck of Barry McLoughlin and Associates, Inc. Their words of wisdom have been an immense help to me.

My co-worker, Janette Andrews, has supported and helped me along the way. Thanks to my colleagues at ScotiaMcLeod for putting up with me for the past 14 years.

Finally, Susan and I are fortunate to be supported by wonderful, loving families. Thanks to our spouses Peggy and Lyon and our children Emily, Meagan, Julia, Adrian, and Nicola. Without you cheering for us, this would still be just a neat idea.

David Cork

Sometimes you get what you want
So be careful what you ask for
Remember what you got

Greg Keelor
Blue Rodeo

1

And Then There Was a Boom

It used to be that hardware stores and I had very little in common. They always overwhelmed me—all those miles of aisles of electrical supplies and plumbing stuff. For Pieter (that's my husband), a hardware store is like a home away from home. The mere smell of the place, that potent combination of new tires and fertilizer, sends him into an altered state.

But I, too, am becoming more comfortable in those hallowed halls. We moved four months ago, leaving behind our modern house in the suburbs with its perfect plumbing and impeccable wiring. We now live in an eighty-five-year-old home in Brookline, near downtown Boston, and the old lady is showing her age. I've been unplugging drains, hooking up the dryer, and fixing sockets. My kids have taken to calling me the Fix-it Lady.

I'm living up to that handle in lots of different ways these days. Our lives needed fixing and, let me tell you, I'm working on it. This past year, our family came too close to going off the rails. Pieter's business hit a hard patch. We could no longer afford that gigantic suburban house. We were becoming irritable with the kids. Finally, the whole thing came down around our ears. We knew we had to make some big changes. That's why we've returned to our roots and come home to this old house in Brookline Village. This is the place where we'd always felt comfortable.

The hardware store anchors our neighborhood. It all happens at Hank's HouseCare, which sits at the corner of Cyprus and Washington Streets. There really is a Hank, and he can tell you how to fix every problem under the sun. With an ever-present smile and free cups of steaming coffee, he's made the store action central—a place where neighbors meet, catch up, maybe indulge in a bit of gossip. Hank's hits its stride during Boston's brutal winters, with its signature nor'easters. Everybody from the surrounding streets, on the premise of buying bags of salt and snow shovels, gathers here and steams up the windows with their chit-chat.

We moved back to Brookline on a frigid day in January. People didn't stop to chat on those blustery days, but over the next couple of months I succeeded in meeting almost all of our neighbors at Hank's. I felt I was getting a good start on fixing things, and needed this human connection, to know my neighbors. I hadn't felt part of a community back in the suburbs and I didn't want to be anonymous any longer. I wanted to feel like a kid again—when I knew who lived in every house, all the way down the street and right around the corners.

When spring was in the air and I could finally leave the house without my winter coat and gloves, I headed to Hank's, list in hand. Time to lay in some gardening supplies. I said my hellos to Hank, then grabbed a cup of coffee and a shopping cart. As I wheeled toward the gardening section, I saw Hazen Armstrong standing in the tool aisle. Even though I hadn't met him, I knew who he was and where he lived. He'd often been the subject of speculation in our winter gab sessions at Hank's.

Hazen was our local mystery man. Every neighborhood has one, I guess—the object of curiosity that positively obsesses people. It was my luck to have him as our neighbor across the street. Rumor had it that he owned a couple of buildings in the area, but no one knew what he did for a living. Someone had heard he had doctorate in philosophy and had been a professor. But it was all just speculation. He wasn't exactly unfriendly, according to the gang at Hank's, just extremely formal and polite. "Courtly" was one description, "old worldly" was another.

After conversations with our neighbors at Hank's, I admit that I became intrigued with Hazen. Thinking about him took my mind off some of the problems nipping at my own heels. He's a walker so it wasn't hard for me to keep an eye on him. Always impeccably dressed, he passed our door a couple of times every day, carrying himself confidently, contentedly. I placed him at about sixty-two years old. My two kids, Malcolm and Emily—

always keen to solve a mystery—were convinced he had either inherited a lot of money or was a lottery winner.

So, here was my mystery man, up close and real. He didn't appear to be shopping for hardware; he was just watching the shoppers, almost as if he were studying them. Never one to stand on ceremony, I decided this was the time to introduce myself even though I feared my outgoing nature might take him by surprise.

"Mr. Armstrong?" He looked up, as if I'd jolted him out of a trance. "Hello. I'm Meredith DeMarco. I've just moved in across the street from you. Sorry, I seem to be interrupting you."

"Not at all. I do some of my best research in hardware stores," he replied, with that perfect diction of an academic. Maybe he is a professor, I thought. And, unlike many Bostonians, he certainly didn't seem shocked by my forward behavior. In fact, he seemed downright happy to see me. "I'm pleased to meet you, Meredith. I've been observing all the activity over at your house. Such a change. It's been so quiet over there for years. Mrs. Mattingley—she lived there before you—was quite elderly, a shut-in for the last few years of her life."

"Yes. We knew Mrs. Mattingley. Her son is a good friend. In fact, we're renting the house from him. He inherited it from his mother."

"Renting? Hmm." My neighbor seemed to retreat into his trance, analyzing this tidbit of information. "That may be a very smart move on your part, possibly even a wise financial decision. Very sound."

A smart financial move? I'd barely met the man and here he was commenting on our financial affairs. I

4

tipped my chin and stared at him. "So, why are we so smart?"

"I'd love to tell you, but I'm in a bit of a hurry," he said, glancing at his watch. "By the way, if you don't know, gardening supplies are over in the next aisle. But I expect I'll see you out in the garden over the next few days. How about chatting then? And please call me Hazen."

This was getting stranger and stranger. Now I knew why this guy obsessed my neighbors. Not only did he say the oddest things, but here we were already on a first-name basis. Still, I liked it. I wanted to know more.

"Hold it. How did you know I was in here to get gardening supplies?"

"That's what you folks are doing these days."

"What do you mean, 'you folks'?"

"You're a baby boomer, right? Boomers have started gardening in a big way. But it's all to be expected. I'm sorry, Meredith. I've got to run or I'll be late. I'll see you in your garden." With that and another glance at his watch, he was off—sort of like the White Rabbit. Hazen Armstrong was more mysterious than ever before.

As I lugged home my hoe, peat, and boxes of bone meal, I wondered whether my life was that predictable. How could Hazen Armstrong presume to tell me what I'd do next? There had been precious little certainty in my life this past year and a half.

—

Eighteen months ago I would never have predicted we'd be back in Brookline. Pieter and I thought we had the good life going—the big house in the suburbs, a minivan (the vehicle of choice back then) and a car, a couple of great vacations every year.

We started our life together here in Brookline. I met Pieter DeMarco at a college party, only two streets away from where we now live. It was pretty close to love at first sight. Pieter is an incurable optimist, and his sunny view of the world attracted me as much as his dark good looks. Though all his friends called him "Pete," I loved his weird first name. Dutch, he told me. It just added to the interesting package that was Pieter DeMarco. Pieter was studying engineering; I was in sociology. We married in 1982, the summer we finished school. Back then, we couldn't wait to get on with our lives.

Before we launched our soon-to-be-brilliant careers, we took the cash we'd received as wedding gifts and traveled for nearly a year. I still laugh when I think of the scolding we got from Pieter's parents as they drove us to the airport. "That money was to be a down payment on a house, not some crazy trip around the world! Your generation needs to know what it is to be poor, then you'd know how to save." Both had been immigrants, his mother from Holland, his father from Italy (which explains his patchwork name). They'd been frugal all their lives, scrimping on necessities, denying themselves luxuries, saving constantly. In their estimation, our generation had lived on Easy Street from day one. Our thinking was different from theirs. We were not wasting our money; we just wanted to experience the four corners of the world while we were still young.

After we returned home to Boston, Pieter went straight to work for a major company, designing software. My own career plans changed dramatically that year. I came home pregnant. (The things you do when you're a kid!) My new career? Mother. Malcolm arrived in 1983, and we decided that I would stay home with our children. Emily was born in 1989. The children were great; we were content and life was sweet.

When the software industry started cooking in the late 1980s, Pieter decided the moment was right to cash in. He and two partners started up their own software firm. At first things were going great. But then the company started running into managerial problems. Too many orders, missed deliveries, servicing glitches, then too few orders. . . .

When the business faltered, everything else came crashing down. We had assumed only financial growth in our lives. The result? We bought into the suburban dream only to find out that it belonged to someone else, not us. We were overextended and mortgaged way over our heads. We thought real estate prices only went one way—up. Pieter's parents were right, I guess. Our generation has been led to believe that the sky was the limit and we bought into that.

In the end, even our real estate let us down. Who would have thought that our house could lose value? We bought it in 1988 for $362,000—and sold it six months ago for $325,000. I was relieved to unload it, even though we lost so much money. That house had come to represent everything that was wrong with our lives, and once the house was gone, I felt we had a clean slate—we were finally back on the right track. But it's been another story for Pieter.

Pieter's definition of success has always been tied tightly to his career. I hadn't realized the extent of that connection until he encountered business troubles. He's been beaten down and he's having a hard time getting up. His energy—once inexhaustible—has dwindled. He's leaning on me, counting on me to be his Fix-it Lady. I'll be damned if I can't turn this thing around. He'd always loved his work before. Now, he has to learn how to make it fun again.

Funny, but I see Pieter as more successful than ever before. He's proving to me that he has the goods to weather hard times. But we have a different perspective. I see an evolution of our lives; he sees only his failure.

And that's how we ended up back in Brookline. We didn't have the cash to buy another house. We had no choice but to rent. And I insisted on being in an established neighborhood. I was tired of wearing the chauffeur's cap. To regain control of our time, I wanted easy access to all the things our family needed. I wanted the kids to be close to their friends and their school (and we'd always been impressed by the quality of Brookline's public schools). I wanted to run my life again, not let it run me.

It was tough when we got here. The first couple of months, I was on automatic pilot, just going through the motions. Everything seemed so diminished—even our street number: 33½ Waverly Avenue. We couldn't even get a whole address. But thank goodness for Hank's and the people in it.

And thank goodness for the kids. Telling the kids was hard. Both Pieter and I felt we had let them down. They were so used to their friends, their neighborhood, and their activities. There have been big changes in their lives. But we've gotten into new activities and taken advantage of the neighborhood, with its old library and beautiful walks. We've had great bike rides along the Charles River—free stuff. The kids have made new friends, and slowly, they turned the corner. They've started to pitch in, helping around the house. Malcolm, in particular, knew something serious was up. He's picked up a few odd jobs around the neighborhood— shoveling snow and walking dogs—and even started buying some of his own clothes (his choice!).

In an odd way, both kids seem to be benefiting from our difficult times. When Pieter and I grew up, we never thought much about money. I remember my parents' stories about the Depression, the austerity—mustard sandwiches, no skates, hand-me-down clothes. It hasn't been that tough for my kids, but there are similarities. Maybe every other generation is alike—our parents were brought up with austerity because of the Depression, our generation had an easy go of it, and now our kids are experiencing challenges because of our financial setback. Through it all, I keep reminding myself how lucky we truly are. We're healthy and so are the kids. We still have enough money to live comfortably. Things could be far worse. Some of the water has spilled out, but the glass is still more than half full.

Sure enough, two days after our chance meeting at the hardware store, Hazen reappeared, this time leaning over my front fence.

"I had a feeling I'd see you out here today," he said, gesturing up to the blue sky. "I'd like to apologize. I could tell by your reaction that I'd seemed presumptuous to you the other day, telling you that renting was clever. It was a purely professional comment. You're the focus of my work—not you personally, of course, but your generation, the baby boomers. You're how I make my living. I study demographics, so I can't help but focus on the boomers. There are almost 77 million of you, you know. And it's time for you to be in the garden."

"But how on earth could you know that?"

"Look at the evidence. First it was Hula Hoops, then downhill skiing, now it's gardening. Whatever your generation hits, it hits hard. Boomers have started to discover gardening. Did you know that consumers spend nearly $30 billion on their lawns and gardens each year? Not surprisingly, lawn and garden sales have been increasing by about 10 percent in each of the past few years. You're the right age for it—you were all born between 1946 and 1964, and you account for 31 percent of the population of this country. Puttering around the garden is your new leisure activity. Nearly 75 percent of American households will be out digging in the dirt this year. That translates into lots of Americans in the garden. And we're only going to see more of you out there. The boomers are moving into solid middle age. And let's face it, the older you get, the more attractive gardening becomes. According to the experts, people over fifty—

and the oldest boomers just hit that golden mark—are the most important consumers of gardening products. I guess it's a lot easier on the joints than jogging."

"Hold it," I said. "Every generation puts its stamp on things." I couldn't decide whether I was intrigued or irritated by this know-it-all and his opinions.

"Not like this one has," he shot back. "This generation caused a demographic disruption. Usually, there's a predictable and regular distribution of different age groups—the proportions between old, young, and middle-aged stay the same. But you boomers threw a monkey wrench into the works. Or rather, your parents did," he chuckled. "The Second World War was over and they wanted to make babies. In the generation ahead of yours, there were less than half the number of births that occurred when you folks started arriving on the scene. And your generation has remained big. It's significantly larger than the next generation. And as a result, you have a dramatic effect on all aspects of our society as you move through."

"Okay, so there's a whole bunch of us," I said. "Why does that make it smart for me to rent instead of own?"

"That's an easy one," Hazen replied. "Real estate is a basic commodity, just like food or clothing. It probably makes sense for people to own a home if they can afford it. Look at the tax perspective, deducting the amount you pay in interest on your mortgage from your taxes and the breaks on capital gains taxes. But don't let the tax breaks cloud the fundamentals of what is an important investment of a significant amount of your hard-earned money. Consider the incredible impact boomers have had on the real estate market. It's affected by supply and demand. You boomers placed a huge demand on the existing housing stock and real estate market when you started to house yourselves. It's no surprise then, that the real estate market started to move in the mid-1970s. That was about thirty years after the birth of the first boomers. By the early 1990s, most of the youngest boomers had purchased homes. So what happened? Just look at the sorry shape of the real estate market back then. The bloom was off the rose. I'd argue that the prices the boomers paid for their homes were drastically inflated."

"But housing prices seem to be heating up again. How do you explain that? We lost a fair amount of money in the real estate market not too long ago," I said.

"No denying the real estate market is hot right now. I think that's due to a combination of low interest rates and pent-up demand—don't forget, there was a while there when not too many people were buying. But I predict this hot spot in the market won't rival what we saw back in the '70s and '80s. Demographics tells us that real estate won't have another wild run-up in the near future because your generation has finished putting pressure on it. They're housed. And the generation following the boomers is small by comparison. It's simple arithmetic—they make up about 17 percent of the population compared to your 31 percent. They can't keep that demand for these houses going." He gestured toward the homes lining the street.

While we were both staring at the Brookline real estate, Malcolm rounded the corner, loping along the sidewalk. I waved.

"Hey, Mom!" he responded.

"It's physically impossible for teenagers to walk like normal people," I whispered to Hazen. He nodded knowingly.

"Hi, Malcolm," I said. "This is Mr. Armstrong. He lives across the street. He's just been telling me that I should be gardening."

"I feel I've chewed your ear off, Meredith. I must say that I enjoy talking to your generation. Next time I want to hear your story. Would you like to join me for a cup of tea tomorrow?"

I nodded.

"Nice meeting you, Malcolm," he said before walking across to his side of the street.

"So did he inherit a lot of money or is he a lottery winner?" Malcolm asked. We laughed together as we walked to the house, arm in arm, my tangled garden forgotten.

—

That evening at dinner, I was bursting to tell Pieter and the kids about my over-the-fence encounter with Hazen.

Family dinners are one of my better Fix-it Lady ideas. Back in the suburbs, we had lost control of our dinner table. Pieter was so busy working, he often wouldn't turn up until long after the dishes were stacked in the dishwasher. I was chauffeuring the kids to Brownies, Scouts, soccer, ballet. You name it, I drove there, and everything seemed to be at opposite ends of the city. Dinnertime became a lost concept. We'd often grab a bag of hamburgers from McDonald's and eat on the run.

That had to change before we no longer even recognized one another on the street. So I decided to reinstate the family meal where we all come together every evening and talk. To get the ball rolling, each of us, in turn, recounts the most interesting thing that happened to us that day. Tonight, Hazen was my topic.

The kids were disappointed that he was not as colorful as they had hoped. Pieter had always prided himself on his intuition, and I could see it kicking in as I talked about Hazen. My husband, I could tell, was intrigued by our opinionated neighbor.

I was really looking forward to that cup of tea.

2

Paradise Lost and Found

I left the house with the kids the next morning at 8:30. Like them, I was off to school. Part of the new DeMarco game plan was that I would return to college. It was time for me to get out to work.

As the bus made its way down Commonwealth Avenue, I wondered if I was doing the right thing. At every stop, more students, loaded with books, clambered on board. They were all healthy, young, and upbeat—talking and laughing about courses, papers, and weekend plans. Anxiety nagged at me. Was I a little too long in the tooth to be slinging a backpack?

During my college days, I'd studied sociology. This time around I wanted to focus on child psychology. And I was feeling pretty lucky to be living in Boston because of one person—Adele Saslove, a member of the psychology department at Boston University. I'd been reading her books on child rearing since Malcolm was born, nodding in agreement with her parenting advice. My kids and I had grown up with her and here I was on the way to meet her, study under her, and maybe even work with her.

My anxiety burst when I finally met with Dr. Saslove. I couldn't believe what I was hearing: she was off for a sabbatical, teaching somewhere in Texas, and I couldn't study with her next year. I left her office in a state of disbelief. This had to be a dream, verging on a nightmare.

I got back on the bus and sagged into my seat. This time, it was emptied of those tall young beauties. As I walked into the house, the phone was ringing.

"Meredith? Hazen here. I'm just putting the kettle on. Will you join me for that cup of tea?"

I didn't even bother to take my jacket off. I needed the warmth of that tea, a dose of reality, and the comfort of being looked after. Expecting the kids home for lunch, I dashed off a note to tell them where I would be and locked the door behind me.

"You look downhearted," said Hazen as he opened the door.

"I am," I replied. "My plans for next fall have just blown up in my face."

"Come on in and tell me about it," he said gently as he ushered me into his living room. I slumped into the corner of a cozy sofa. Ever the snoop, I cast my eye around the room. Every inch of the place was comfortable—thick Oriental carpets, welcoming armchairs, bookcases lining one wall. I'd never been to an English gentlemen's club, but this room seemed as if it belonged in London. The room actually looked like Hazen.

I told Hazen my woes. "So there goes my year," I finished.

"Hold it right there," he said. "Surely there are plenty of other fish in the sea. Just because that professor isn't around doesn't mean you should put your plans on hold. As luck would have it, I know someone at B.U. who you should meet. Her name is Ruth Schneider. She's a sociology professor."

"Sociology," I repeated. "I have my degree in sociology. But I did that years ago. How could she help me?"

"She's a smart woman—and not just book smart. She's been around. She knows how colleges work. She might have some good advice for you about courses and professors. I was just speaking to her yesterday and she was moaning about the fact that her research assistant just up and quit to go traveling in Tibet. Give her a call. Who knows? You might just land some part-time work from her." Hazen moved into the kitchen, where I could hear him rattling tea cups and pouring water.

"You know, I just might be interested," I said. I was losing that saggy feeling already. A little extra cash couldn't hurt, and it might be a good way of testing the waters. A research job might give me a feel about how I'd manage on campus with all that glorious youth. I pulled myself out of the deep sofa and tailed Hazen.

He was filling a tray with cups, tea, and a plateful of pecan squares. "There are going to be many in your generation who will be thinking of new careers in the next few years—some by choice, some have no choice. The economy is changing," he said. He opened the refrigerator and poured some milk into a small silver jug.

"You're not alone, you know," he continued. "One in four college students is a boomer. Granted, plenty of them are part-timers, but the best-educated generation in history is still hitting the books."

"And here I was feeling too old to go back to school," I mused.

He turned back to face me. "Two phenomena are currently shaping our society," he began. "First, we are going through a dramatic technology surge. Second, we have a huge and aging bulge in our population, courtesy of our middle-aged baby boom. These two facts are having quite an effect on our economy. The speed of change is staggering."

"So is that why you know so much about my generation?" I asked.

"Yes. My work focuses on the shape of the nation's population."

"Its shape?"

"I look at the distribution of the U.S. population—the number of children, middle-aged people, seniors, that sort of thing. And our population looks like a well-fed python." He chuckled.

"A python! You mean a snake?" I was having trouble keeping up.

"Yes, a python. Now imagine that the python has just swallowed a pig. The boomers are the pig. The python represents our economy. This image explains perfectly what's going on right now."

"A pig and a python?" I still couldn't fathom his argument.

"Precisely. We have a huge bulge of boomers in the middle of the python. Smaller generations are on each end. But it wasn't always this way, and the shape of the python will change again before the boomers are finished with it. Think of it. The python is trying to digest his lunch just as the boom is constantly aging and progressing along his length."

"And Pieter and I are in the middle of the python. Right?"

"You've got it. There, you've just heard the introduction of a little talk I call 'The Pig and the Python.'"

"Talking about the boom is your job?"

"I'm a financial consultant. For the past twenty years, I've advised business and private investors on the impact your generation has been having. But I wasn't always consumed by the boom. I did have a previous life, and it's not nearly as mysterious as the neighbors would tell you. Want to hear it?"

"You're right about the neighbors. Sure, tell me." I wanted to hear about someone who had reinvented his life because that was where I was headed. Starting over.

Hazen started in. "I had just finished my doctorate in philosophy at Brown and landed a job as a professor there. That was back in the mid-1960s. Wild times in those days. The colleges were bursting at the seams. Lots of unrest on campus. You were probably a young teenager, but you remember Kent State, the generation gap, the Doors, 'love is all you need.' The times they were a-changin'. During my first year of teaching, I went to a lecture by a visiting professor. He spoke about the social unrest happening across the country. The baby boom had caused this unrest, he reasoned. The mere existence of this huge generation was disrupting our society. Every generation that had gone before the boom had been assimilated by society. But your generation, because of its great size, had the ability to force society to change to accommodate it. I began thinking about his arguments. If the baby boom was causing this much ruckus, wouldn't they continue to have effects? What would those effects be? I started to pick up all the material I could on the boom. Before I knew it, I was obsessed with the topic. It became the focus of my work. The boom has changed my life. That one lecture was a revelation. It changed my destiny, you might say."

"So how did you get from teaching philosophy at Brown to talking to investors about the baby boom?" I asked.

"Even while I was teaching, I was always a capitalist at heart. I knew I wanted to get out into the business world. The baby boom proved to be my meal ticket. One day I picked up a research report from a major brokerage firm. One kernel of information hit me right between the eyes. It was so clear that I didn't even need to think about it. I knew what my future business would be."

"Sort of like an epiphany or a defining moment? What was it?" It was obvious that this stuff really excited Hazen. I was starting to get hooked too.

Hazen laughed heartily. "You promise you won't think me crazy?"

I nodded—but secretly I thought he might be a little off.

"Baby food. Remember the Gerber baby?"

Now I was certain he was crazy.

"The report concerned consumer products, and the information that hit me focused on the food industry. There was a passing reference to the fact that the surge in births immediately after the war had caused Gerber's sales to double between 1948 and 1950. That gem of information was the start of my work."

"Sorry, I just don't get the connection," I said.

"You started out as a baby, right? So did everybody in your gigantic generation. Gerber, a company that catered to the needs of all of you babies, was one of the first to feel the effects of the baby boom. Here's what excited me. Gerber was only the beginning. There were plenty more products and companies yet to benefit from the boom. I realized that all these babies—the oldest were in their early twenties when I had this revelation about the boom—were going to continue to have a huge impact as they continued to age and make their way through society. They weren't just causing social unrest. The baby boom was causing economic unrest too! And the economic effects of the boom will not end until they die. This generation will continue to have an enormous influence as they age and hit other products and markets."

"But hasn't society always been this way? Population has always expanded," I argued.

"Not like this. The baby boom is very different from previous patterns of population growth. Two factors set it apart from previous generations. First is what we've already discussed—the large size of the boomer group relative to the generation before it and following it. Second, the generation in front of the boom—those born between 1933 and 1945—is relatively small because of one critical factor: the Depression. Boomers put tremendous pressure on the assets of this smaller generation and consumer products when they were born. Look at the Gerber baby."

"So my generation is an aberration?" I asked.

"Exactly. That's what gives the boom its power."

"And the Gerber baby told you all this?"

"Well, I did have to think about it a bit. It dawned on me that as the boomers aged, not only would they influence the markets and society but, more importantly, I could predict what they'd influence. I could turn that information to my financial advantage. The key is predictability."

"Right," I said. "You mentioned that the other day at the hardware store. I must admit I didn't like having my future predicted like that. It's unsettling."

"You're not the first person to tell me that. A lot of people think life is completely unpredictable. They like to take life as it comes. I call them the 'random walkers.' They stroll through life just waiting for the next thing to come along, no rhyme or reason. In fact, life's not like that at all. You can predict the next step because of the very size of your generation."

"Okay, I'm game. Tell me more."

"Have you ever heard of the law of large numbers?"

"Vaguely, but I couldn't explain it," I answered.

"The law of large numbers states that you can predict events if the survey of people or things—whatever you're looking at—is large enough. Let me give you an example." He reached into his pocket, and with a dramatic flourish, pulled out a shiny silver dollar. Crazy he might be, but there was no denying Hazen's entertainment value. His actions were so polished, it was obvious that he had done this demonstration dozens of times before.

He cleared his throat. "Now, if I flip this dollar in the air, can you predict with certainty whether it'll be heads or tails?"

"No."

"If I flip it ten times, what would you expect? Maybe six heads to four tails or maybe three heads and seven tails. Kind of hard to predict, isn't it? But if I was to stand here and flip this coin 1,000 times, you can be fairly certain that each side will come up about 500 times. That's predictable—the law of large numbers."

"Okay, I'm with you so far," I said. But where was this guy going with this demonstration?

"Can you apply the law of large numbers to people?" Hazen asked. "Individuals may not be that predictable, but are large numbers of people predictable?"

"I don't know. Are they?"

"Think about it. There's one industry that uses the law of large numbers to predict something rather amazing about people. Actuaries predict very accurately when we will die. The insurance industry could not survive without these predictions about people as a large group. Now, here's what excites me about the law of large numbers. If you can predict when people will die using the law of large numbers, you can also predict when those people will buy their first car, move into their first home.

I can predict when they will put pressure on the consumer products they'll need—and it's not baby food any longer; it's walking shoes and eyeglasses. But I can also predict the pressure this group will put on financial markets, when they'll influence inflation rates and interest rates. You name it. So are these things predictable? Of course they are." He pocketed his dollar and picked up the tea tray.

"Come into the living room. Let's have our tea before it gets cold. As usual, I get on a roll when I'm talking about the boom. I could go on all day."

I followed him. "And this demographic stuff has worked for you?"

"It's never failed me. I've positioned my investments wisely by watching the bulge work its way through the python. The pig and the python—that's the ticket." He poured the tea. "Milk or sugar?" he asked.

Now it was my turn to be lost in a trance. This was interesting stuff. "Just a drop of milk, thanks. This information could be used in a lot of different ways, couldn't it?" My thoughts had immediately turned to Pieter and his work. He was always casting about for new product ideas. It seemed to me that this knowledge could be useful for him.

"Yes, it has many other uses."

"You know, Hazen, I'd really like you to meet my husband." I paused, carefully considering what I'd say next, but I felt so comfortable with Hazen that I found myself confiding in him. "Pieter's having some trouble getting his business up and running. I think he'd be interested in hearing what you have to say. Things have been a bit uncertain for him recently."

"I'm sure I can put a degree of certainty back into his world."

—

I was full of information at our dinner table that evening—the Gerber baby, Ruth Schneider, the pig and the python. Spurred on by Hazen's stories of the 1960s, Pieter and I started reminiscing about bell bottoms, the Monkees, long hair, and flower power. The kids had a good laugh at our expense ("You mean you wore striped bell bottoms, Dad? Oh, yuk!").

More important, Pieter made the same comment I had made at Hazen's. While we were loading the dishwasher, he said, "You know, this demographic information could have plenty of uses. More than just entertaining the kids. I'd like to meet this guy."

"I'm sure he'd make you a cup of tea." I smiled my Fix-it Lady smile.

3

Midlife Angst

I was standing face-to-face with Jerry Garcia, wondering whether I was in the right place. I fumbled in my shoulder bag, searching for the scrap of paper on which I had written Ruth Schneider's office number. Surely a member of the sociology department at Boston University would not have a poster of the late great lead singer of the Grateful Dead fitted up in groovy Haight-Ashbury gear taped to her door. The number on the door, however, did match the one Ruth had given me over the phone.

Acting on Hazen's advice, I had called Ruth. A warm, deep voice answered. I nervously told her who I was and that Hazen had suggested I call her.

"That Hazen." She gave a long, rich chuckle. "He's always full of advice, isn't he? Did he mention that I need a researcher?"

I told her that yes, he had, and that I was very interested in the position, but felt I should explain my circumstances. "Just so you know—I'm not a student yet,"

I added. "I mean, I was a student back in the '70s. Now I'm going back to school after staying home with my kids. And I'll be turning thirty-eight this summer." Why had I babbled on like that? This woman didn't need to know my age!

"Perfect. That couldn't be more perfect. I'm looking for someone about your age to help out with my work," Ruth said. "Listen, I have a light teaching load tomorrow. Why don't you stop by in the morning?" Maybe I'd said the right thing after all.

So, here I was, face-to-face with a wild-eyed Jerry Garcia, when the door swung open.

"I thought I heard someone out here. You must be Meredith. I'm Ruth. Come on in." She offered her hand and delivered a firm handshake. I guessed her to be in her fifties. She was definitely an original. Her long, thick hair, slightly greying, was loosely pulled back into a ponytail. Her clothes were funky—a cherry-red suede vest and charcoal ankle-length skirt. A dramatic silver locket hung on a thick chain around her neck. This was a woman who knew who she was, and I coveted that look.

As I followed Ruth into her office, I swallowed my anxious feelings. I had a strong and immediate intuition about this woman. I was going to get this job. We were going to work together well. And I could tell I would like her.

"So, I see you're a Grateful Dead fan," I said.

"I don't think of myself as a fan. I'm just part of a movement," Ruth replied. "I see Jerry's music as a kind of river flowing through the heart of America. I admit to being pulled along by his current. I was just part of the flock. You know, he said: 'We're just happy freaks, man.' I like that. There's nothing wrong with being happy or a bit different from the rest of the crowd." She scooped some papers off a chair and motioned for me to sit down.

I looked around her office. It was a jumble of books, papers, and scores of photos—photos in frames, tacked on a bulletin board, taped to the walls. And every picture featured smiling people—arms linked, hugging, embracing.

"You sure seem to know a lot of people. I don't think I've ever seen so many photos in one place," I said.

Ruth slowly surveyed the room. "Windows of the soul, don't you think? These little scraps of memory are my strength. They take me to the good times and good people of my life." Ruth fell quiet for a moment.

I pointed to a shelf full of pictures, clearly all of the same boy, charting his progress from an infant to a toddler and on up to a tall, gawky teenager. "That person is obviously special to you. Is he your son?" I asked.

Ruth pulled one of the frames down, hugging it to her chest. "Ah, my pride and joy. This is my son, Dylan."

With a quick mental calculation, I guessed Dylan to be in his mid-twenties. "Was he named after Bob? That must have been a popular name when he was born."

Ruth smiled. "No, he's not named after the musician. He's named after the poet Dylan Thomas. You know— 'Do not go gentle into that good night.' Good guess, though. You ask good questions, Meredith. Now it's my turn. Would you like some coffee? Sorry, I'm behind the times—it's not Starbucks." She shrugged, reaching for a thermos sitting on her desk.

"I'd love some," I answered. "Just a drop of milk, please."

She handed me a mug of steaming coffee. "This is highly unusual for me—I don't usually hire people on the spot but I've got a hunch that you'd be perfect for this research job, Meredith. You have a natural curiosity. Do you realize that you've asked me a string of questions? You've been here less than five minutes and you already know about my passion for Dylan Thomas. You're exactly who I need. I'm looking for an interviewer who can pose questions and elicit meaningful responses from a group of middle-aged people. You have the personality for it."

"And here I thought I was just a natural-born snoop," I said. We both smiled.

"Tell me how you know Hazen Armstrong," she asked. Now the conversation was getting down to business.

"He lives across the street," I replied.

"So, has he performed his silver dollar routine for you yet?" Ruth chuckled.

"Yes, I've seen that demonstration. And I was impressed by it."

"I shouldn't make fun of Hazen. It's just that I've seen that show more times than I can count. Hazen and I share a common passion, you see. The baby boom is central to the work we do. But our approaches are radically different. For Hazen, the boom is a business opportunity. For me, it's an academic pursuit. I focus my attention on the individuals who make up your generation."

"I never knew that my generation was so influential, so important, until I met the two of you," I said.

"It was no accident that Hazen would send you my way. Your age makes you a good fit for the work I'm doing."

"So my being nearly forty will be useful to your work?"

"It's music to my ears. I think the people that I need interviewed will open up to you," she replied.

"It seems such a lucky coincidence that I studied sociology in university," I said.

"Just all part of the plan, I guess." Ruth looked straight at me. "So, tell me about yourself, Meredith. Let's see how we'll work together."

I told her about my college studies, my kids, and the recent changes in my life. Funny, I didn't feel reluctant to tell her about my need for a change. In fact, I felt compelled to speak openly to her. She seemed so interested in me. "I feel it's been a long time since I used my head. I need to start thinking about things again. I want to feel that I am contributing to my life, not letting life sweep me along." Ruth listened intently, not moving until I was finished.

"Let me tell you a bit about me—to see if you're interested in my work," she said, settling into her chair. "I was doing my graduate work at Berkeley back in the mid-1960s and I was sniffing around for a thesis topic for my doctorate. It suddenly hit me—there were way more young kids around than when I was young. Back in the 1950s, maternity wards were full to overflowing, elementary schools were opening at an astonishing clip. Then, in the 1960s, the campuses were crammed with young students. This horde of children was raging its way through society. Heady times back then—the Vietnam War in full throttle, social unrest, lots of change. There was my topic, right in front of my nose. The baby boom! My thesis was entitled 'The Role of the Postwar Cohort in Altering the Societal Status Quo.'"

This stuff seemed to have the same powerful effect on Ruth as it did on Hazen. "Okay. I'm ready for the translation. What was your thesis really about?" It was my turn to laugh; Ruth joined in.

"I took myself so much more seriously in those days," she said. "The postwar cohort is the baby boom. And they did alter the status quo. Many believe they changed the world."

"But isn't the world always changing?" I asked. My nervousness had evaporated. I felt as invigorated by Ruth as I had by Hazen. It felt good using my head this way. It reminded me of my years at college—those late-night sessions in the dorm talking about the meaning of life (always accompanied by pizza).

"The world does change," Ruth said slowly. "You're right. Usually, though, young generations are easily assimilated into society. But your generation is so abnormally large and dominant in comparison to others, that it is impossible for it to be absorbed. By setting society's agenda, the boom was able to alter society, reordering it in its own image. Take a look around. Why do you think we keep hearing about the Beatles these days? Why do you think all those nostalgia radio stations are at the top of the ratings? Your generation is the reason."

"Is the boom a good thing? Are all these changes good?" I asked.

"I guess the answer depends on who you are. I think the boomers have profited, but the youngest boomers and the generation that follows the boom complain about being hard done by. In my professional opinion, change is necessary not only for the advancement but for the survival of a society. Have you heard of Joseph Schumpeter?"

I shook my head.

Ruth took a sip of coffee and launched in again. "Schumpeter was an economist in the last century. What he had to say is particularly relevant now, as we face a new millennium. He coined the phrase 'creative destruction.' He told about how old machines were replaced with new ones. The process was a painful one, for both economies and workers, as change came along. But, he argued, change meant progress. If our society is to move forward, change is necessary, inevitable. I see the same thing happening with our population. You could say that the baby boom is creatively destroying the old world order in favor of a new one. The boom is a vehicle of change in our society. And yes, there has been pain and dislocation associated with the boom, and that will continue. But in the long run, this generation will take our society to a higher level of diversity and development. So, I guess I'd have to say that the changes the boom has wrought are good." Ruth sat back in her chair.

It was exciting to watch and listen to someone so passionate about her work. "How did the boom bring you from California to Boston?" I asked.

"I finished my doctorate in 1970 and started to look around for teaching opportunities. There was an interesting job here."

"And this is where you met the infamous Hazen Armstrong?"

Ruth laughed again. "Not long after I arrived here, a friend at the college told me he had another friend who was obsessed by the boom. He took the two of us sailing in Boston Harbor and watched Hazen and me do battle. Our first meeting was quite electric. But despite our differences, we've been close friends ever since."

"But I thought the two of you shared the same ideas."

Ruth smiled. "We share a study of the same phenomenon, but our interests and approaches to the boom are totally different. The boom is like a prism. What it shows you depends on how you hold it to the light. Hazen is a born capitalist. He wants to know where the boomers are headed so he can make informed investment decisions. I just want to know what makes the boomers tick and how they will affect the larger society around them. I was born before the boom. I've lived as an outsider looking in at this influential generation. I'm watching the boom hit middle age and experience the midlife angst that comes with that period of development. They're all trying to figure out how to live the second half of their lives. I think the boom's uncertainty goes a long way to explaining the introspective mood that our country is mired in right now. In fact, that's why I need a researcher. I'm working on how the boom's position in life affects society's view of itself."

Ruth made such good sense. She certainly had me pegged. So many things were happening in my life, and I could see no clear path to the future. Things used to be so easy—time to go to college, time to have kids, time to buy the house in the suburbs. Things just weren't so clear to me any longer.

"I think you're right," I told her. "I find myself trying to sort through what to think, what to do, how to react."

Ruth slowly nodded her head. "Meredith, the answers are out there for you. All the ideas and philosophies we need to make our lives work exist today. You need only to find the ones that will help you make it through."

She took another long sip of coffee. The room was quiet. I could hear the ticking of an old-fashioned mantel clock sitting on her filing cabinet. An intercom blurted something incomprehensible out in the hallway.

"We could work together, Meredith. We'd both learn some useful things from one another, I think. I had a feeling from our phone conversation that you could handle this job. Synchronicity, that's what it is. Coincidences tend to happen when you need them. Right now, we could both use the skills the other has to offer."

I felt the satisfying feeling of things falling into place. A good job had just landed in my lap, along with the opportunity to work with this wise, kind woman. I couldn't wait to share my good news with Pieter and the kids.

We arranged the details for a meeting during the next week and my visit to B.U.'s personnel department to finalize the paperwork of my contract. Ruth gave me some background reading material for the research she was working on. As I was stuffing everything into my shoulder bag, my shopping list dropped out. I picked it up and told Ruth that my next stop was the craft store. I explained that Emily and I would be making plasticine snakes for a Brownie project on reptiles.

"I remember those days well. You're in classic domestic feminist mode—juggling the demands of family and career. Difficult balancing act, isn't it?"

"A domestic feminist. I've never heard that expression before. I take it that's a good thing to be?" I picked up my bag and headed for the door.

"Absolutely. I look forward to seeing you next week." Ruth waved and closed the door gently as I stepped into the hallway.

I looked back at Jerry Garcia, staring at me from the door. What a long strange trip it had been. I was so excited, I thought I'd break into song.

—

That evening, I made our family's favorite dinner— tortellini and a huge tossed salad.

"Sit down, everybody. I have big news tonight," I called, putting dinner on the table.

The three of them straggled in from the living room, where Pieter had been helping the kids with their homework.

"What is it, Mom? Why are you so happy about dinner?" asked Emily.

"It's not dinner that's making me happy, ladybird. I've got a job at Boston University. A really good one with a professor named Ruth Schneider," I sang, while doing a crazy little dance around the dining-room table. It had been a long time since I'd felt so good.

"That's great, Mom," said Malcolm.

"Am I going to have to go to an after-school program?" Emily asked, her eyes widening at that prospect.

"No, it's part time. I'll only work while you're at school."

My husband was oddly quiet. "Pieter, what do you think?" I asked.

"Well, I'd like to hear more about it," he answered cautiously. I sensed Pieter envied my joy. Oh, Pieter, please be happy for me, I thought, as I launched into a description of Ruth, her office, and her work.

At the end of my story, I could see I'd won him over. Pieter then stood with his glass of cranberry juice in hand. Ever since the kids were old enough to drink from a glass, we'd celebrated our successes with a family toast. "I'd like to propose a toast to Mom."

The kids rose. "To Mom," they shouted in unison. Ruth was right. It was good being a domestic feminist.

4

Think!

After coffee on Saturday morning, I persuaded Pieter to walk up to Hank's with me. I knew he was down when I had to work so hard at interesting my hardware store aficionado in a visit to one of his favorite places. Pieter had wandered into Hank's a couple of times since we'd moved back to Brookline but only to pick up the bare essentials—some nails, picture hooks, a furnace filter. He hadn't soaked up the flavor of Hank's like I had. He resisted becoming a full-fledged member of our new neighborhood. In the same way, Pieter wasn't interested in fixing up our new home; for him, the house was a rental unit.

Hank, cheerful as ever, was near the door when we walked in. I poured two cups of coffee and handed one to Pieter. He eyed it suspiciously. "You told me we were going to be here for a minute," he said.

"Relax, it's Saturday. I've got a few things to pick up," I said, pulling my list from my jeans pocket. "You could help me, you know. Look," I said, pointing to my list. "I'd like to paint the upstairs bathroom. I can't stand that bubblegum pink. Help me choose a new color."

"I really don't think it makes sense to be putting so much money and time into a house that we're renting," he replied.

I could feel my blood pressure rising. Pieter was lucky we were in a public place. We'd had a number of heated discussions on this topic. Pieter has this thing about owning land. He often preached about the tax benefits of owning a home and how we should buy again, as soon as we were able. For him, land is a real, tangible investment—as he says, "They don't make it any more." This time, I decided to take a level-headed, logical approach to the issue. Will Rogers be damned!

Remembering what Hazen had told me about renting as opposed to owning real estate, I said: "Hazen says we're making a wise move by renting until we know where we're headed. Boomers are housed. Buying a house may not be the best investment we can make with our money. We shouldn't buy another house until it makes good financial sense. Maybe we should stay in this rental for a while. And if that's the case, I want to paint the damn bathroom." Better stop here, I thought. I could feel myself getting riled.

Just at that moment, I spied my savior down the aisle in gardening supplies, pushing a fertilizer spreader. I walked over to him.

"Hi, Hazen. Do you have a moment? I'd like you to meet my husband, Pieter," I said.

"I can't talk long—I'm working today—but I'd love to meet Pieter."

"Were your ears burning?" I asked as we walked back to Pieter. "We were just talking about your ideas about the baby boom. You know, the benefits of renting as opposed to buying a home." I introduced Hazen to my husband.

"Call me Pete," said Pieter, shaking hands with Hazen. Hazen launched in. "I was just returning this spreader to Hank. He lets me borrow some of his equipment in exchange for a few tips on what your generation is up to. You boomers are his bread and butter."

"Meredith has told me you're full of predictions about what the future holds, Hazen. I'd be interested in hearing more." I was surprised. Pieter wasn't usually so forthright.

"I'd love to talk because I think we could come up with a few ideas for your business that you might find interesting. Unfortunately, it can't be right now. I'm off to a meeting."

This was my chance to get these two talking and I wasn't going to miss it. "Hazen, would you be free for dinner this evening—say, at seven? I'm roasting a chicken. And I almost forgot the most important thing—thanks for introducing me to Ruth. I got the job!"

"So I heard. I spoke with Ruth yesterday and she thanked me for sending you her way. As for dinner, I'd like that. I have no plans. I'll see you at seven and I'll bring the wine."

"Don't forget to bring your silver dollar," I said.

"I always carry it for luck," he said with a chuckle.

Pieter and I worked our way through my list—he even relented on the paint! On our way home, he was quiet, lost in his thoughts.

"Hazen's an interesting man, isn't he?" I said, as we neared home.

"He seems to have that 'I've figured it all out' sense about him," replied Pieter.

"You'll have to meet Ruth. She's like that too. They're two peas in a pod, both so confident and both so interested in the baby boom."

We reached home, eager to begin preparations for the evening's dinner party.

——

Promptly at 7:00, the doorbell rang. Emily rushed to open the door and take a good look at the mysterious Hazen Armstrong. Both kids were disappointed that there wasn't something nefarious about our neighbor. Stepping into the hallway, Hazen introduced himself to Emily while handing me a bouquet of spring flowers and a bottle of wine.

"One of the advantages of being older," he explained. "You always have a few good vintages kicking around for these occasions."

"I think we can put this to good use," said Pieter, walking in to greet Hazen. Pieter looked at the kids and gave them the nod. "Okay, guys—one TV show, then it's off to your beds. You can read a bit and it's lights out by nine-thirty." After a bit of moaning and groaning they ran off, arguing about who would choose the show. They both knew this was a special evening for Pieter and me.

"Come on in, Hazen. How does a scotch sound? We have a great single malt around someplace," said Pieter as we moved into the living room.

"We're going to hit it off perfectly, Pieter. Scotch is my drink. I'm not surprised you've got a good bottle of scotch in your liquor cabinet. The trend for alcohol consumption has been in a marked decline for the past fifteen years or so. Boomers are growing up and drinking less, especially hard liquor. Quality is replacing quantity—and you boomers are now ready and able to part with the money to enjoy exotic and expensive premium products," replied Hazen, settling into the sofa.

"Interesting. You're right. Fifteen years ago, I'd never consider buying a bottle of scotch like this," Pieter continued, pouring our drinks. "Meredith has been telling me about your work. Let me see if I've got it straight. You study our generation to see what the next economic trends will be. Then you use that information to determine where and how you should invest your money." Pieter handed a glass to Hazen.

"Thank you," said Hazen, taking a deep drink. "Your generation is my passion. The generations on either side of yours are small in comparison to the boom. So you folks become the ultimate impact players in our economy."

Pieter was obviously intrigued, the way he gets when the discussion turns to hi-tech issues.

"Right, the pig and the python concept. Meredith explained that to me. But what makes the impact of the boom so special, so different from other generations?"

Hazen seemed to anticipate this question. "Your generation acts like a predator unleashed on a new environment. Let me give you an example. Many years ago in Jamaica, rats were a big problem. To get rid of the rats, mongooses were imported to the island. A mongoose is a natural predator, and the rats were gone in no time. But then the mongoose turned its predatory nature toward chickens. Not so good."

I was confused by this little tale and I could tell Pieter hadn't followed it either. "Are boomers like the mongoose?" I asked.

"Precisely, Meredith. The mongoose doesn't eat chickens on purpose. He's not doing it to be bad or evil. It's his nature. He's simply reacting and adapting to the environment he's been placed in."

"So, the baby boomers are a bunch of passive predators, reacting to the environment we've found ourselves in," I said.

"Passive predators. I like that expression, Meredith. Mind if I pilfer it to use in my presentations? Your generation is a group of passive predators. You change the landscape simply by being here."

"You're on a roll, Hazen. How about another scotch?" asked Pieter. Hazen nodded and Pieter rose, picking up Hazen's glass.

Hazen continued, "I was serious this morning when I said I'd been thinking about how the boom could help your business, Pieter."

"Do you know much about the software industry?" Pieter asked.

"Actually, I know next to nothing about the technical aspects of it, but I do know a great deal about your generation and the products it wants and needs. That's always the starting point in all of my work," Hazen explained, leaning across the coffee table to take his glass from Pieter.

Pieter, I knew, would be skeptical about taking advice from someone who admitted ignorance of the hi-tech business. "How could you help my business with that information?" he asked.

"For over forty years, your generation has been making or breaking products. Take a look at the Chrysler minivan. In 1979, Lee Iacocca was in front of Congress, cap in hand, begging them to save his company. A decade later, Chrysler was smashing all its profit and sales numbers. Either Iacocca is a genius and figured out the market, or he got lucky. In any event, Chrysler was first to the market with a minivan and the boomers bought them like hotcakes. Voilà! Chrysler was saved."

"You're suggesting that the boom saved Chrysler?" Pieter asked.

"Well, think about who drives those things. The minivan was the boomer's vehicle of choice, perfect for ferrying around a young family. Appeal to boomers and you've got the market licked. It's like I said—the vast size of your generation dictates the success or failure of a product. Plus, your generation is always on the lookout for new products. Times change and, while many basic requirements stay the same, your generation doesn't necessarily have the same wants or needs as your parents'."

"What do you mean the minivan 'was' our vehicle of choice? We still have one," challenged Pieter.

"Let's look at the big picture," replied Hazen. "Remember station wagons?"

"Sure, all our parents had one," I said.

"Right. That was the product of your parents. Like I said, you boomers are always watching the horizon for the next new thing. You might be doing a lot of the same things your parents did at your age—raising kids, holding down a job—but you can't be seen driving your dad's car! Minivans—the soccer mom's vehicle of choice—now outsell station wagons five to one. But boomers can be a fickle lot. Now minivan sales are slumping. Boomers' kids are growing up and boomers aren't so worried about carpooling as having a safe, durable car for all of their teenagers to drive. You wait—minivans are fast losing their prime spot to the sport utility vehicle."

"I see. You're saying that the key to the success of any product is to tempt the boomers. So, if we can tempt boomers with a software product and tap into the boomer market, we're guaranteed success."

"Absolutely. And if I were you, I'd be thinking about time. Time is the one item that your generation doesn't have enough of. Just look at the two of you." Hazen animatedly gestured toward us. "You're busy with the kids. Meredith, I see you driving them here and there. Pieter, I know you work extremely long hours. And it's only going to get busier when Meredith starts working with Ruth. Your family is not uncommon. Ask any boomer. They need more time."

Boy, he was on the money with that comment. I felt I was always shouting "Hurry up. We're going to be late!" at Malcolm and Emily. I never remembered my parents feeling the time crunch the way Pieter and I do.

"It's the 'build the better mousetrap' idea," Hazen continued. "If you could deliver a software product that somehow gave your generation more time, I think you'd have a real winner."

Pieter sat, glass held halfway to his lips. The wheels were turning. "That's certainly how all successful inventors think," he said. "They try to fill a need in society."

"But here's the exciting thing for you, Pieter. You're in the right place at the right time. You're definitely in the right market. Just look at the interest we're showing in computers. In 1984, only 8 percent of households had a computer. By 1995, that number had jumped to nearly 35 percent and it's still growing. Over the next couple of years, it has the potential to reach a whopping 50 percent. Families with school-age kids spend approximately twice as much as the average household spends on computers. Lots of boomers now have kids in the school system, and there are still plenty of projects to input into the computer. If you time your product to what the boom is currently interested in, you'll hit pay dirt."

"Time," repeated Pieter. "We're all running out of time. Let me think about that one. When I've got some ideas, can I run them past you, Hazen?"

"Absolutely. Depending on the product, I might even be interested in providing some venture capital."

This was going even better than I could have hoped. Before putting the dinner on the table, I took a quick run upstairs to check on the kids. I could hear Pieter and Hazen moving to the kitchen, checking on the chicken. By the time I got back downstairs, Pieter was carving the bird and they were well into another debate. This time it was the merits of economists.

"Why do you think economists always get it wrong?" Hazen was certainly enthusiastic about this topic. "They don't study people," he said heatedly, without waiting for a response from Pieter. "They have abstract models and theorems but seem to forget that it's people who cause the economy to move one way or another. They should pay closer attention to the study of demographics," he harrumphed.

"What do middle-aged boomers mean for the economy?" asked Pieter, deftly slicing the chicken and arranging it on a plate.

Hazen put his glass down on the counter and cleared his throat. "Pieter, our future couldn't look brighter because of the boomers. Think about it. Boomers were once extremely expensive creatures. When you were young, you needed to be educated. That was a huge drain on the economy—building schools and colleges, hiring teachers. Then you moved into your first jobs. Again, you needed training. It's only now as boomers move into their middle years that they are producing at full tilt. Now, the economy can reap the money that's been invested in the boom over the years."

"But that's not what we're reading in the newspapers and magazines," Pieter answered. "Even stories talking about how great the economy is doing these days usually contain a line or two warning us that the whole thing is going to go bust."

"I couldn't agree more. The news can be quite a depressing affair. But the media tend to report what's happening today. They're not looking down the road like I am. The boom is fast approaching middle age. And I predict that it's going to be a time of savings and investment for this generation. The big spending years are behind you—most boomers have the house and the car. Now, it's time to save. And most baby boomers are also entering their peak earning years. I predict a golden age." He laughed, raising his glass aloft.

I jumped into the conversation. "I wish I could feel as optimistic as you, Hazen. You're so upbeat. Pieter's business has drained our nest egg. It's been tough for us."

Hazen nodded. "You've had a bit of a hard time, but as soon as you're over the hump—and you will be—your optimism will return. Business can be tough. You need to hang in and you need to have a plan."

"I guess we always thought our ship would come in," Pieter explained. "I thought planning was for the average person, not for me."

Hazen smiled. "Pieter, everybody needs a plan to get their financial house in order. Everybody, from the most successful right down to the common guy. It's all about fundamentals."

"What do you mean by fundamentals?" asked Pieter.

"You've both heard of the baseball player Cal Ripken, Jr.?" Hazen replied.

We both nodded in response.

"Well, think about what makes him so successful, so consistently successful."

"He's a naturally talented guy," Pieter ventured.

"It's not just natural talent. There are plenty of guys with more talent than Ripken. Some are probably pumping gas in Hoboken, New Jersey, as we speak. It's fundamentals. It's planning. Cal Ripken practices his craft every day of the year. He goes over and over it until it's mechanical."

"So how does that relate to our finances?" Pieter asked.

This was obviously the response Hazen was waiting for. "Boomers need to practice the fundamentals of their lives, and that includes financial fundamentals. You have to plan to get ahead. You have to think."

"Well," I said, "we've thought about what we'll need in the next few years moneywise. We've talked a lot about the money we'll need to send the kids to college."

"That's a good start, but it's not enough," said Hazen. "What you need is a good financial plan, a detailed, well-thought-out plan that focuses not only on your future obligations but also on how you're going to get the money to pay for those obligations. You can put one together—you just need to think long and hard about it."

I jumped in again. "I guess you're right, Hazen. But I don't think Pieter and I really know how to put a plan like that together."

Hazen took a sip of wine. "That's not surprising. You're not alone. We've done a poor job of educating ourselves about financial matters. When you were young, did your parents ever talk to you about money and finances?"

Pieter and I looked at one another and started to laugh.

"There wasn't a lot of money in either of our families," Pieter said. "There wasn't a lot to talk about. Quite frankly, our parents didn't know much about finances."

"I think your parents would have preferred to talk to you about sex than money," said Hazen. We all laughed. "Your parents could afford to avoid the subject," said Hazen, serious again. "They were lucky. Your generation is significantly larger than theirs, and all of you forced up the prices of their assets."

I could see where Hazen was going with this. "So what you're saying is that we boomers created wealth for our parents."

Hazen nodded. "Exactly. The boomers pushed interest rates up and bid up the prices of their parents' real estate. But the boomers have a problem. There isn't a large generation behind them pushing up the prices of traditional assets like real estate. Boomers are going to have to look elsewhere for their investments. And boomers are going to need to plan more than their parents did."

This conversation unsettled me. The more Hazen spoke, the more I began to think about what Pieter and I needed to do. For so much of our lives we'd been reacting to what went on around us, expecting that we'd get by. The events of the past year had taught us that we had to do better than simply react to things as they came up. Hazen was right—we needed a plan.

"Did I ever tell you why I was so interested in both of you?" Hazen asked, changing the subject.

I shook my head. "No, you didn't."

"The first time we met, I could sense that you had a genuine interest in me. I liked your curiosity. I could tell you were different from some of the neighbors. Plus, you're a boomer, and I'm always interested in boomers."

Dinner floated along, a pleasant evening of talk and laughter. During coffee, Hazen cleared his throat and his look turned serious. "I hesitate to mention it because I don't want you to feel pressured to accept my invitation. But I'm going to be delivering my demographics presentation at the Marriott downtown on Monday night. I'd really like you both to see it. It would give you a better idea about my work and would probably help both of you in your work. Actually, I think Ruth might be there, Meredith. I count on her feedback."

Pieter and I looked at one another. "I think I can find a sitter for the kids," I said. We smiled. "Okay, we'll be there."

5

The Shape of Things to Come

Ruth phoned first thing Monday morning asking if I'd like to see some new boomer material she thought might be useful for the interviews I'd be conducting. By 9:00 I was on the bus, backpack on my shoulder, heading for school and happy for the diversion. This was much better than tackling the loads of laundry sitting in the basement.

"Good morning, Mr. Garcia," I said under my breath as I knocked on Ruth's office door.

"Come on in," shouted Ruth from behind the door. "Meredith, I'm so excited. You won't believe the amount of new boomer material one of my students has collected off the Internet. People are really starting to pay attention to the power of the boom. I think this stuff is going to be extremely helpful to us."

As I entered the room, my gaze immediately fell on two file folders stuffed full of computer printouts. Yikes! My eyes widened. That laundry was going to have to wait a day or two; I had plenty of reading ahead of me. Ruth, ever observant, noticed my reaction.

"Here. Sit down," she said, pulling a chair out of the corner. "You don't have to read everything right now, you know. I'd suggest skimming it and focusing on the important stuff." She started pulling sheets from the folders. "Look, here's a couple of articles on recreational vehicles and the boomers, one from *Time* and another from something called *RV Business*. Interesting pieces, I'm sure, but not something we'll need to focus on."

She handed them to me. I skimmed the summary at the beginning of the *RV Business* article. It told RV dealers how to snare the interest of the "lucrative baby boomer generation," nearly 80 million strong. According to the *Time* article, sales of RVs in 1996 hit a record $12.4 billion, 50 percent higher than at the beginning of the 1990s. No doubt about this one—boomers are driving the RV market skyward.

"Actually, Hazen would probably like to read these," Ruth continued. "He's always interested in finding industries that'll benefit from the boom." I returned the articles to her, and she slipped them back into the file, flipped through a few more, and pulled out another. "But here's something we can definitely use. It's by Debra Goldman in a publication called *Adweek*. It's about boomers facing up to their own mortality and the early-1990s recession. Listen to this: 'By a twist of fate, this recession gripped the nation just as the boomers were experiencing their first intimations of mortality. Somehow, this spectre of death has contributed to a morbid consumer psychology, a pessimism that has transformed a garden-variety economic downturn into a mortal blow to the American dream.'"

"You know, that makes good sense," I said. "As this big group ages, there's going to be more talk than ever before about growing older."

"And most people get more cautious as they age. Back in the early 1980s, this country endured a rotten recession, but unlike the 1990s recession, we snapped out of that one consumer confidence intact—ready to spend, spend, spend. I think that can be explained, in large part, by the age of the boom back then. The majority of the boomers were in their thirties and busy forming households, buying stuff to fill their new houses and apartments, thinking about having babies. We bought our economy out of the recession. Then, in the '90s we were again plunged into a recession, but it was ten years later and the boomers were ten years older. That time around, even though the 1990s recession was technically shorter than that of the 1980s, we just couldn't shake the pessimism that enveloped us. Now, it looks as if our economy is chugging along full throttle, but there's still an underlying fear that it's all going to evaporate. Here, I want to show you something else from *Time*." She picked up a photocopied article from her desk. "This piece is all about our burgeoning economy, yet it has an entire section devoted to telling readers that they better not get used to economic and social health—the good times are going to be gone by the end of the 1990s. To my mind, this is all about the funk that baby boomers are wallowing in. I want us to study this phenomenon." She closed the files and handed them to me. We were quiet for a moment. I stared out Ruth's window, feeling older and a bit wiser.

"Thanks, Ruth. I'll get started on these this afternoon. Speaking of baby boomers, are you going to Hazen's talk tonight?" I asked.

"I usually try to go to his talks here in Boston. I always pick up a new nugget of information from him. But don't tell him that," she laughed. "It'd go straight to his head. Actually, he likes to hear my feedback. Constructive criticism only, however." She laughed again, a rich, throaty chuckle.

"We'll see you there, then. Pieter and I plan to go."

"Good. I think you two could benefit from what he has to say. You know, he won't give you all the answers. In fact, he poses the questions the audience should be addressing. You'll have to decide how to use the information he provides you with, but knowledge about demographics gives you one very useful tool for investing. I guarantee you'll come away with some insights into the way you should be conducting your financial affairs."

"We could use that," I said, remembering our dinner-party conversation.

"It's never too late to learn something new. If there's one thing I've learned in my long life, you need to keep growing—intellectually, spiritually, every way," responded Ruth. She glanced at her watch. "Meredith, I don't want to hustle you out the door, but I've got a class in five minutes and it's a quick walk from here. I've got to fly. Don't forget our meeting on Friday morning." She started pulling on a jacket.

I packed the bulging file folders into my backpack, feeling very much a part of an interesting new world. Yes, it was going to be a lot of work reading all this stuff, but I was going to learn things that would have practical application in my own life. An investment in myself! I liked that. I hadn't done that in a while.

—

Pieter and I didn't want to be late for Hazen's presentation so we sat down to an early dinner Monday evening. Given his mysterious reputation, the kids were curious about Hazen's talk.

"But what's it about? How can somebody talk about money? What will Hazen say? Why are you going?" The questions kept coming, and Pieter and I realized once again that we really didn't have a solid grasp on money matters.

On the way to the hotel, Pieter and I revisited our dinner-table conversation with the kids. "You know, we're a lot like our parents," I commented. "Just like them, we don't have the skills or knowledge to talk to our children about finances."

I cast my memory back to the mealtime conversations of my childhood. We talked about politics, books, school projects, family stuff—but never ever about money. Dad was a schoolteacher, Mom stayed home with the six of us. Six of us! My parents took their part in creating the baby boom seriously. Then again, there never was much money to talk about, what with six kids and a teacher's salary. Mom and Dad had counted on Dad's pension. Too bad it was such a short retirement. They died within a year of one another. The year Emily was born, Dad's heart gave out on him. The next year, Mom, a lifelong smoker, was diagnosed with lung cancer. She was gone in six months. God, I missed them. The six of us were left with the house. It still had a small mortgage, taken out to finance our weddings. Each of us ended up with about $25,000. Pieter and I decided to put it in T-bonds for the kids' education. We felt that investing in bonds would be what Mom and Dad would want us to do.

"But we're not alone, you know," Pieter said, rousing me from my thoughts. We couldn't think of any of our friends who'd attended financial seminars. We'd seen lots of advertisements in the newspaper for these things, but never considered attending before—the whole thing just seemed too complicated. We never seemed to find the time to think about our financial future. And that made me nervous. Something had to be done. Ultimately, we'd have to save for our retirement—nobody else was going to do it for us. And now there was so much talk about how Social Security wouldn't be there for us like it had for our parents' generation. The whole thing had become a vicious circle. Not enough time, too much anxiety, too many complicated decisions. Instead, we had taken the easy route. We procrastinated. Tonight we were going to alter that course.

The hotel was hopping when we arrived. We estimated about 500 people were here to listen to Hazen. The audience was mixed. Lots of older folks, but also plenty of people our age who looked a lot like us. I glanced around for Ruth but couldn't spot her.

"Let's go in and grab a couple of seats. It's going to be packed," said Pieter.

At our seats, we found a folder full of articles. Pieter started pulling things out.

"Hey look, it's Hazen," he said, showing me an article from a local newspaper with a photo of our neighbor smiling from the page.

I skimmed it quickly. "It quotes Hazen here. 'Demographics doesn't specifically tell you the future. It is a tool so you can start developing things that give you better information than the next person.' That's exactly what Ruth told me this morning. . . . "

We had just begun leafing through the remaining articles and graphs when a well-dressed woman walked to the front of the room. Smiling and confident, she clipped a microphone on her jacket lapel and introduced herself as the local manager of the financial planning firm sponsoring the seminar.

"Ladies and gentlemen, we are pleased to introduce you to a man who's been called 'The People Prophet.' Hazen Armstrong is a private consultant who has studied the impact of the baby boom for the past twenty years. He interprets population trends to the benefit of both himself and his clients, large institutional investors. Tonight, he will share some of his insights with us. Ladies and gentlemen, Hazen Armstrong."

Hazen shook the woman's hand and took his place at the front of the room. He looked out over the audience and smiled a slow, calm smile. I was impressed. He'd obviously done this before and was in control of the place.

"About fifty years ago, something funny happened in North America," Hazen started in, his voice strong and well modulated. "I'd like to begin by reading you a quote:

'The war was over. People wanted to settle down and calmly blow their way out of years of rationing. They wanted to bake sugary cakes, burn gas, go to church together, get rich and make babies.' That was written by Annie Dillard, an American writer, reminiscing about her 1950s childhood. If you were around in the 1950s and the 1960s, you too know about these babies. Interestingly, the demographers of the day thought the first couple of years were just a catch-up period. We'd quickly get back into our old patterns. But people were obviously doing something they liked. The catch-up went on for twenty years. Now, we've all heard about this phenomenon: the baby boom. But what you may not have heard is how to turn this unusual event to your financial advantage."

The room was quiet. Hazen commanded his listeners' attention.

"The tough times of the Depression resulted in a significant drop in the number of births in this country. This means that the generation preceding the baby boom is particularly small. This generation, many of whom are parents of boomers, is positively dwarfed by the boomers it produced. Let's take a look at the statistics. In 1921, the fertility rate—that's the average number of children born to a woman—stood at about 3.3. By the mid-1930s it had dropped to about 2.2. By 1959, the fertility rate had skyrocketed to almost 4. Today it's back down to the low 2s." He stopped briefly, allowing these details to sink in.

"Where does this leave us? We have a small generation, followed by an extremely large one, followed by another relatively small generation. This is a demographic aberration, and it is guaranteed to have profound effects. It will cause fluctuations in the values of things we buy or hold. These fluctuations in values are the theme of my chat tonight." Again he paused, looking around the audience.

"When the babies of the boom grew up, they started to buy things. Things like houses. And guess what? They were buying houses from their parents' generation. They put pressure on that generation's assets. Why? Because so many of them were chasing a limited number of assets. The boomers acted like predators." Hazen paused. "Passive predators."

He caught my eye and smiled. I'd have to bring up the issue of the royalty tomorrow.

"These passive predators don't put pressure on commodities because they are aggressive or mean-spirited. No, boomers pressure things because their generation is so huge. They started with hospitals, moved to schools, and on to money, real estate, and—now—mutual funds. And there is never enough of a commodity when they first hit it."

Hazen took a sip of water. "Now, what do I mean by a commodity? These are the assets that we need to carry on our daily lives—food, real estate, money, stocks and bonds, jobs. The law of supply and demand governs commodities. When the boomers show up, wanting to buy commodities, they show up rapidly and in enormous numbers. Remember supply and demand? Well, boomer demand far outstrips supply in every commodity they hit. The result? Higher prices for whatever commodity the boomers want or need. The story is repeated in every market: rapid, strong pressure on short supplies by a large, demanding group of passive predators."

I was pleased at my turn of phrase. I looked around the audience—still engrossed.

"So how can we use this information to our financial advantage? Let me give you a brief definition of the term *demographics* because I think it will help you see where I'm heading. Demographics is the statistical study of human populations; it boils down to simple numerical facts. Facts such as how many teenagers we've got and how many senior citizens; how many people were born in a given year and how many people died; how many immigrants arrived in the U.S. and how many people left. This knowledge could give us great power if we cared to use it. We could prepare for increases in school enrollments, shortages of young workers, and bursts in demand for housing, all of which are predictable years in advance."

Again Hazen paused, facing the audience.

"Predictability. Think about that for a moment. Imagine that the world is predictable." Hazen became contemplative. I knew where he was headed with this one. He spoke about the "random walkers"—those folks who firmly believe life is completely unpredictable. Then he spoke about actuaries and their work predicting when we as a group are going to die. He quickly explained the law of large numbers and left the audience with a question.

"If actuaries can use the law of large numbers to predict when we are going to die, surely we can predict many other future events? Events such as when people will land their first job, buy their first car, rent their first apartment, buy their first mutual fund. So far we've talked about demographics, commodities, and pre-dictability—and the connection between the three. Now I want to focus on three specific commodities: money, real estate, and the stock market. Each of these plays an in-tegral role in our financial well-being. Money affects all of our decisions. We use interest rates to measure and price this commodity. Watching interest rates is a bit of preventive medicine we should all use. Real estate is the commodity the boomers have just hit. The stock market is where they're headed next. I want to talk about each of these commodities in the context of supply and de-mand."

Hazen walked over to a laptop computer and pushed a button. On an overhead screen, up flashed a smiling baby. A gentle but nervous laugh rippled through the audience. What was going on here?

"I'd like to introduce you to the Gerber baby. This little fellow can tell you a lot about your future—and interest rates, real estate, and the stock market." I suddenly felt smug knowing what was coming next.

"Do you know that Gerber's sales doubled between 1948 and 1950? But that only makes sense. We were ex-periencing a baby boom and babies must eat. In fact, Gerber's sales kept surging over the next fifteen years. Then came 1965. The babies stopped coming quite so fast. The boom was over. And so was the run on Gerber, forcing the company to diversify into other businesses, including life insurance and child care. So what can the

Gerber baby tell you? The Gerber baby is an early warning system. Think about it. Because of its product, Gerber saw the boom first. If you knew that Gerber was going to have a great twenty-year run between 1946 and 1965, you could tell that the school system would be hopping between the 1950s and the 1970s. Better yet, you would know that interest rates would take off and be above average in the 1970s, peaking in the 1980s, because boomers were growing up and beginning to borrow money. It comes as no surprise that, as boomers aged, interest rates would settle down in the 1990s. You would know that real estate prices would surge in the late-1970s and 1980s as boomers housed themselves. And you'd know that investment markets would start to take off in the 1990s as the boomers started to focus on their retirement plans. That little Gerber baby could have told you all of this way back in the 1950s. That's predictability."

I could tell the crowd was catching on here. Pieter sat beside me nodding. Hazen walked into the center of the audience.

"Okay, let's talk money and interest rates." I laughed to myself. Now Hazen was starting to come across like the financial version of Phil Donahue, working the crowd. "Can you remember what this country was like in the '60s? It wasn't all flower power and hippies, you know. The United States was a fairly conservative place back then. Pretty stodgy, actually. We saved. Then the '70s rolled around and all hell broke loose. Our savings rate plummeted, our debt levels skyrocketed. If you looked at the statistics, it appeared as if we'd all lost our minds. Well, in fact, not much had changed. The boomers burst into the market in the 1970s, skewing the statistics as they always do with their enormous numbers. They were only kids back in the '60s, but by the '70s this huge group of passive predators started to join the economy as adults—with adult wants and needs." The audience chuckled.

"They were eager to start purchasing coveted consumer items: a stereo, a car, and, a little later on, a house. This huge group turned to the banks to finance their purchases, and their borrowing activities placed unparalleled demands on money. Like a horde of locusts, they hit money markets hard and forced rates through the roof," he said, gesturing toward the ceiling.

Hazen walked back to his laptop and replaced the Gerber baby with a graph showing the ratio of spenders versus savers. "Back in the '60s, we had just about as many savers as spenders. Savers are generally categorized as folks aged forty-five to fifty-four; spenders are younger people just starting out, aged twenty-five to thirty-four. You borrow when you're young; you pay it back as you get older. For years we were in equilibrium—as many savers as spenders. Then in the late '70s, the adult boomers began to arrive on the scene and the number of spenders took off while the number of savers stayed pretty constant. So much for our equilibrium. The boom showed up and we moved into a period of unparalleled disequilibrium. This period peaked in the mid-1980s. Look: we had almost two spenders for every saver in the American economy. This phenomenon put huge pressure on money.

"Remember supply and demand. Just as they had pushed other commodities, the boom was now pressuring the price of money. Like any product for which demand exceeds supply, the price of money rose. Those were the years when we saw our interest rates hit 20 percent. Since the mid-1980s, we've been moving back toward a position of equilibrium between savers and spenders. Apart from a couple of blips, we've also been watching interest rates fall steadily since then.

"Be forewarned—we will soon be entering another period of disequilibrium. But this time interest rates won't be going up. Why? Over the next fifteen years, as the boomers age and go into savings mode, we're going to see more savers than spenders. We'll have an oversupply of money in the economy. I'll say it again. Remember supply and demand. I predict that rates will be destined to stay low for years. This time around, spenders will stay constant. It's the savers—courtesy of the boom—who will explode in numbers."

Once again, he left the laptop and walked toward the audience. "I'm often asked whether we have lost the capacity to save. People point to the marked decline in our savings rate—it's fallen from 12 percent back in the 1950s to 4 percent in the 1990s. I have several responses to that question. My short answer is 'No'—you just wait until boomers swing into savings. Don't forget that the 1990s recession cramped saving in this country. Between the late-1980s and the mid-1990s, the real median household income dropped like a stone—down over 7 percent between 1989 and 1993. Financially strapped boomers, young adults during this period and struggling through a tough recession, had a tough time putting money away. But the recession is finally behind us and, for many, incomes are beginning to move upward very slowly. There are a couple of other points that need to be made about our savings rate."

Hazen paused, then strolled confidently across the stage. "I want to talk about two things: economists and seniors. Both are impacting our notion of savings in this country, but in very different ways. The usual measure of savings is what people put away as a percentage of after-tax income. But this measure doesn't tell us the whole story—far from it. Economists are now telling us that a more accurate yardstick of our financial cushion is to look at our net financial assets. Looking at the increase in value of our stocks, bonds, and homes—our stash of savings—gives us a bigger picture than a simple focus on what we tuck away from our incomes. Surprise! An examination of our net financial assets reveals that, even though many of us have weathered hard times recently, we continue to have a healthier financial cushion than standard measures of the savings rate indicate. And courtesy of the boomers, that cushion is really going to fatten up over the next couple of decades."

Again, he stopped speaking for a moment, allowing his ideas to sink in. "Now, let's look at the impact seniors are having on savings. Seventy-year-olds in the 1990s consume more relative to thirty-year-olds. Back in the 1960s, seniors consumed significantly less than the younger generation. There's a relatively simple explanation for this change. Older folks are feeling positively flush these days. The past thirty years have seen increases in government benefits to the elderly, and they have a positive outlook about Social Security—it will continue to provide for them, easing their retirements. In addition, this group reaped healthy returns on their real estate and higher than normal rates on their CDs for several years. Add it all up, and I think we should call this group 'The Lucky Ones.' Of course, it didn't hurt to have an enormous generation coming up behind them, bidding up their assets and funding Social Security. Boomers won't have that luck, and that's the main reason that I see savings becoming a key priority in the future. It has to, or else the boomers are going to be in rough financial straits when it comes time for them to retire. And I know that plenty of you know you need to be saving now for retirement in the future. Less than 30 percent of adults in their thirties believe they will ever receive Social Security benefits. Boomers know they need to save. In the future, wealth won't just happen; it will have to be planned. It's simple mathematics. The generation behind the boom is small—it won't bid up the boomers' assets and happily fund Social Security. Here's your early warning signal—start saving now if you ever want to stop working!"

Hazen strode across the stage. "Enough serious news. Let's talk about the good news. And low interest rates are very good news—if you can take advantage of them. Low rates will keep plenty of commodities buoyant, and they could even throw a little life back into the real estate market. You'll recall that one of my themes is predictability. I'd suggest that even the real estate market is predictable."

Now he had everybody's attention. This was a pretty well-heeled crowd. I figured they'd all had their real estate ups and downs, like Pieter and me.

"I promised you I'd talk about the future of real estate. Here's my advice. Think about the real estate market in the same way you'd think about any other commodity. What do I mean? For too long, real estate has been our sacred cow, a no-brainer investment. You put money in, you made money. Simple. But not any more. If the boom is moving at a segment of the real estate market, prices in that segment will go up. If the boom is selling a segment, it will go down. And boomers are changing as they hit middle age. There are several key migrations taking place. Downsizing is one of them. Back in the 1980s, 'he who dies with the most stuff wins' was the ideology that drove many boomers. As they age, boomers today are trying to make sense of their lives—owning lots of stuff doesn't seem nearly as important as it once did. It doesn't seem to make them any happier. Buying only what you need, not what you want, does make sense. The move to technology is another critical migration pattern. Many folks have discovered they can run a business quite nicely in their basement in Boise, Idaho, and perhaps have a higher quality of life. They have technology—computers, faxes, modems—to thank for that. Location, location, location is not as critical for certain businesses as it once was.

"I mentioned earlier that the boom is significantly larger than the generation ahead of it. That made for quite an impact when boomers started to buy up homes from the members of that older generation. Now they are housed and real estate has slowed significantly because the baby bust generation, those born between 1965 and 1978, which follows the boom, is less than three-quarters the size of the boom. This means that the supply of younger first-time buyers has dropped off. That raises two key points. Stay away from starter homes. Think vacation homes instead. Once again, consider the boom. Here's an interesting statistic on second homes. Back in 1990, only 25.5 percent of Americans felt they had a chance of buying a weekend retreat within the next ten years. By 1995, that number had jumped to over 60 percent. The aging boomers are solidly behind those numbers."

Pieter looked over at me and mouthed, "I told you so." I smiled, thinking about our cottage and the bone of contention it had been between us. Something still didn't seem right—renting a home in the city while owning that splendid luxury: a cottage up in New Hampshire. When our finances were stretched to the limit, Pieter had made me vow that we wouldn't sell the family cottage. His parents had given it to us several years back. They were finding it too difficult to manage the upkeep. So we struck a deal. They'd give us title to the place—a sort of early inheritance—and we'd let them have it to themselves for a month each summer. Between taxes and supplies, the place cost us each year about as much as a two-week vacation in Florida would set us back. Suddenly, I realized I was lost in my thoughts about our Spofford Lake place. When I came to, I heard Hazen discussing the stock market. He'd moved back to the center of the crowd.

"Imagine," he was saying, "that there had been a law twenty-five years ago stating that you could buy a home only in a few American cities. That's right. You couldn't buy a home in Cleveland or Tampa or Seattle and not even here in Boston. Think of what that would do to real estate prices in those cities. It's a pretty silly concept—you can buy land anywhere, right? Now, think about the stock market. There's no law that states you have to buy blue chip stocks in New York. But in this country, it's a fact that the only blue chip stock markets we have are located in New York, plus a few other cities, including Philadelphia, Chicago, and San Francisco. By blue chip, I mean stock of an active, nationally known company that has a track record of dividend payments and other good investment qualities. Remember what the boom did to real estate—all across America. Now imagine the power surging toward those few stock markets. Think of the pressure on this commodity as institutional investors show up in earnest. What do I mean by institutional investors? Banks, trusts, pension funds, insurance companies, and, of course, we can't overlook stock-based mutual funds. In the past six years—going back to the early-1990s when the boomers started showing up in financial markets—mutual funds have exploded, their assets increasing fivefold. And this is just the beginning." Hazen paused, lifting his hands, palms upward, and looking around the audience. Heads were nodding in agreement.

"Look at what's going on around us. We're all being coaxed to plan our own retirements. And we're given generous tax incentives to do this. We've all heard of

401(k), IRA, and Keogh accounts. There are definite tax advantages if you contribute to these accounts. In the long run, you'll end up with more income. Plus, earnings on investments held in these accounts aren't taxed so long as the investment is kept in them. Everybody's agreed, putting investments into a retirement account is a good thing. Now, what do we put into them? We really have only two choices: fixed-income instruments, such as certificates of deposit, treasury bills, and bonds, or equities—that's the stock market. We've already predicted that interest rates will be staying low for the next few years, so that takes the blush off fixed-income investments like CDs. That leaves all of us staring at the stock market. And we've seen the power of the boom when it hits a market."

Hazen returned to his laptop and pulled up a chart showing the boom in mutual funds over the past decade. My mind drifted off again. The idea of investing our hard-earned dollars in the stock market unnerved me. I'd never bought a stock in my life. Never looked at the pages and pages of stock tables in the newspaper. How was I ever going to figure this one out? I knew we had some money in an IRA, but I wasn't sure how much or in what it was invested. I refocused just as Hazen was finishing up.

"I know the stock market has not been the first investment choice of everyone, but it should be. This is where investors are headed now. We should think of the baby boom as an early warning system. By 1946, the Depression and the war were over. The men had come home and America began to experience a massive baby boom. In fact, by 1957 there were almost twice as many live births in the U.S. as there had been during the depths of the Depression. But babies grow up and they head off to school. . . ."

Hazen walked across the front of the room. "In the state of Massachusetts—back in 1944 before the boomers began to arrive on the scene—113,852 children between the ages of five and seven headed off to school. By 1954, the boomers had started their educations and 177,321 five- to seven-year-olds filled the classrooms. And, ten years later, when things really started to heat up, 211,663 little ones crammed into classes. But the boomers kept moving along . . . In 1976, they were joining the economy in a big way. They needed loans to start their lives. That kicked off unprecedented levels of interest rates and inflation. In 1986, the country's largest generation was more or less housed and the hot real estate markets were showing signs of cooling. In 1996, the boomers turned their collective attention to their retirement needs. This will have a dramatic impact on investment markets for years to come. And in 2006—well, I don't want to give away too much. I want you to come back for my next seminar." A chuckle rippled through the audience, and Hazen laughed along with them.

"I'm sorry that I can't take any questions tonight. I understand that we'll be breaking for coffee now and I'd be happy to talk to you individually. But before I let you go, I want to leave you with a thought. It's time to learn. If you're an average American, you probably don't know too much about the financial markets. Well, now's the time to brush up on your knowledge.

I'm part of a generation that was small and successful by default. The cavalry rode into town, in the form of the huge baby-boom generation, and it bid everything up. My generation profited. This won't happen to your generation. Success in the future will come only to those who study the changing environment and invest accordingly. Thank you for your attention this evening."

Applause rolled through the audience. I caught Ruth's eye and beckoned to her. She smiled, waved, and began walking through the crowd toward us.

She extended her hand to Pieter and they introduced themselves. I could see Pieter was impressed by this animated woman.

Ruth began, "I was hoping the three of us could have a quick drink in the hotel bar but, unfortunately, I can't stay and chat. Guess who flew in unexpectedly this afternoon?" She was so excited, she didn't wait for my reply. "My son, Dylan. I want to get home and have dinner with him. He told me he'd make us a curry. A pleasure, Pieter. See you Friday, Meredith." With that, she flew off, leaving Pieter and me staring at one another.

"I'm tired, Pieter," I said. "Hazen gave me a lot to think about tonight."

"Yeah, I feel the same way. But you know, I'm excited about finally getting a grip on what we need to do to save for the future. I'm getting darn close to forty—it's time to be thinking about what's ahead," he said. "Can't put it off much longer. Why don't we go and say goodbye to Hazen?"

We looked around the room only to see Hazen being mobbed in a corner. He had at least twenty people patiently waiting to speak to him.

"We're lucky. We can ask him questions any time—we know where he lives," I said, taking Pieter's hand in mine. "Let's go home."

6

The Craft of Life

When I arrived at Ruth's office on Friday morning, I could hear music coming from behind her door. James Taylor, if I wasn't mistaken. I poked my head around her door. "Hey, have you forsaken Jerry?"

Ruth laughed. "No, this is work. Did you know James Taylor has a new album out?" She picked up a CD case and pointed to the photograph of a sepia-tone, serious-looking Taylor.

"Hey, he's getting on," I said.

"Precisely," replied Ruth. "At forty-nine, he's one of the older boomers and Taylor is singing to all those boomers following behind him. Boomers are still listening to their old rock 'n' roll favorites, including the Grateful Dead, I might add. Nearly 60 percent of boomers like to listen to rock. After all these years, Mick Jagger can still pack them in. But they like to listen to 'new' rock too—something that reflects where they are in their lives today. That's what Taylor delivers." She walked over to the CD player and clicked James off.

"And that, I believe, is what accounts for his continued popularity," she continued. "The boomers are now middle-aged and they've seen a bit of life. They're growing up, and in the process they've been kicked around the block once or twice—job problems, divorce, kid trouble. Taylor's songs fill the bill. His music focuses on the highly personal story: love and loss, birth and death, friends, family. The thing that interests me is how rock music has changed over the past decade. It used to have a younger, harder edge. It's growing up with the boomers and shifting gears, becoming more pensive and mature along the way. James Taylor's trip through life is shared by many boomers—starting with the hippie and drug thing, moving into the failed marriage experience, parenting challenges, and recently his brother and a couple of close friends have died."

"Sounds kind of depressing. Who'd want to listen to all that on an album?" I asked.

"That's Taylor's genius—he's got an optimistic spin on life's tough lessons. Despite all he's been through, he sees a promising future for your generation. Boomers want to hear good news—and they're also at the stage where they want to know that life has some meaning. Why do you think we're hearing so much about spirituality these days? Taylor's got a very good grip on the state of your collective mind," replied Ruth. She reached for a newspaper clipping on the corner of her desk.

"Here's something I found in *The New York Times* recently. It quotes Taylor talking about the boom. Here it is: 'Our generation took up so much space we didn't have to refer to anything in the past.'"

"That's a claim for the power of the boom if I ever heard one," I said.

"Exactly. The boomers are on center stage and they're going to stay there for awhile. Taylor goes on to say that he's optimistic about the future of our culture—when you folks are in your fifties and sixties and still healthy and kicking. This album should do very well, courtesy of demographics," she replied, popping the CD out of the machine and snapping it into its case.

"The strength of the boom seems to turn up every-where—from selling cars to listening to music," I said.

"Well, Hazen and I have focused on the boom so we do have a clearer perspective than most," she responded. "But it always amazes me that people don't appreciate the influence of the boomer generation. Every generation possesses opinions different from those of the genera-tions on either side, but never before has one generation had the power to impose its opinions on society like the mammoth baby boom generation. You heard Hazen's take on the boom the other night. I might as well give you mine." Ruth sat down in her chair, pushing her reading glasses to the top of her head.

"The baby boom sets the agenda in this country. There, that's it in a nutshell. Let me give you a current example. Look at Social Security. You can't open a news-paper without reading about the Social Security crisis—how it's going to run out of money by the time we all retire. Why is Social Security such a big deal right now? Simple—the baby boom. Social Security worked just fine for many years, but now it's facing this huge generation that's going to start retiring in the 2010s. The current structure of Social Security—payroll taxes collected from today's workers first go to pay the benefits of today's retirees—just isn't going to work when the baby boomers start to retire. By 2012, just as your generation starts hitting its golden years, Social Security will be spending more than it collects. Experts estimate that today's Social Security surplus—the 'trust fund'—will be gone by 2029. There'll be way too many retired boomers and too few workers footing the bill. So, something must be done to accommodate the boom. The pressure is now on boomers to look after themselves. I'd suggest—just to be on the safe side—that boomers start saving in order to provide their own nest egg. But stress on Social Security is only one example. The baby boom sets the agenda socially, culturally, financially, and economically in this country, and it's been that way since the boom arrived on the scene. They're strengthening their grip on that agenda as they age. Now they're at a point in their lives when they are starting to take their roles at the helm of companies and governments. And they're bringing their opinions and interests with them to those exalted positions."

I nodded. Ruth pushed her chair back, crossing her legs, looking positively professorial. I realized I was listening to a segment of a lecture: "Introduction to the Boom."

"Did you know that there are two groups of boomers, what demographers call two cohorts?" she asked.

"Cohorts! Sounds like people who commit crimes to-gether," I said.

"Partly right, actually. Cohorts do things together. For demographers, a cohort is a group of people born during a defined time period. They share a slice of history and many of the same life experiences, tastes, and prefer-ences. In my lectures I quote a writer named Frederick Buechner: 'They have come from the same beginning. They have seen the same sights along the way. They are bound for the same end and they will get there about the same time. They are your *compagnons de voyage*.' I love that expression. Think about it—you can probably re-member where you were when you heard that JFK was shot," she said.

"Just barely," I replied. "I remember my mother watch-ing the TV and crying her eyes out."

"That's a memory that you share with all the others in your cohort. The cohort that follows you can't know what you know. You and your *compagnons de voyage* were shaped by that experience. In the same way, your children and the members of their generation will share the memory of where they were when they heard Princess Diana had died. That memory will give shape to their lives."

"But how does the baby boom divide into two groups? I thought it was one gigantic group," I said.

"Partly right again. It's one gigantic generation. Generations are measured in the time it takes a person to grow up and have children—that's about twenty to twenty-five years. But within the baby boom generation, there are two distinct cohorts. The front cohort was born between 1946 and the mid-1950s. The second are those born in the second half of the 1950s and the first half of the 1960s. The cohort chasm that divides the two is the end of the Vietnam War and the beginning of the Watergate era. The first group of boomers came of age in the 1960s. They shared the positive slice of history that Kennedy's Camelot brought this country. They thought they could change the world. The second group knew that wouldn't happen. They came of age watching their world unravel as the economy started losing its luster, seeing the Watergate fiasco. In fact, Taylor has a great song, 'Line 'Em Up,' on his new album, all about Richard Nixon and 'his shifty little eye.' Their slice of history wasn't nearly as optimistic as that experienced by the older boomers. It's now twenty-five years later and some of that cynicism hasn't gone away. In fact, I'd argue that the younger boomer cohort resents the older one, sort of like you'd resent an older sibling—the older one gets everything and you're left with hand-me-downs. You could say that the first cohort was out to change the world, whereas the second cohort saw its role as saving the world from the first."

"Interesting you should say that," I commented. "I've got five brothers and sisters. I've always envied my older brothers. Everything seemed so easy for them—jobs, buying a house, you name it. But when I look at my youngest sister, I see someone who is very concerned about her future. Even though she's younger, she's by far the most conservative of us all."

"That's not surprising," replied Ruth. "There's a lot of diversity in this generation. But the power of the two cohorts of the boomer generation comes from looking at all of them together. And there are many things that everyone does, despite our view of the world. I believe we're on the brink of seeing some interesting new developments as the first cohort moves into solid middle age. They're starting to turn fifty and they have fifty-year-old problems. Their health isn't as good as it once was, they've got to think about retirement, and their kids have left home. These are fundamental lifestyle changes. How is this affecting them and their view of the world? I'd suggest they've realized that perhaps they can't change the world." We both laughed at that.

"But that realization doesn't mean they'll become like their mothers and fathers before them. Although they'll do many of the same things, a fifty-year-old today won't be exactly like a fifty-year-old of his parents' generation. That's the importance of understanding cohorts. Even though the cohort grows older, it can never shed the core values it acquired while it was growing up. For anyone trying to sell things, this is particularly valuable information. Are you finding this boring? Do you mind if I give you another example?" she asked.

This animated woman couldn't be boring if she tried. "No, I've never heard this stuff before. I'd actually like to know how those marketers look at me," I replied.

"Okay. Do you drink beer?" Ruth asked.

"On occasion. I've always loved the taste of a cold beer."

"Do you drink as much beer as you did in your college days?"

I laughed. "Are you kidding? My body's not as young as it used to be, and I've got to get up every morning with two kids. No, my big beer-drinking days are behind me, I'm afraid."

"Well, the beer market has gone down the drain in this country. The traditional breweries like Coors and Miller are having a hard time increasing their market share. All you boomers have grown up and aren't drinking twelve beers at one sitting! So the brewers have changed how and what they sell to your generation. You've heard of Anheuser-Busch?"

I nodded. "Who hasn't? I've been known to lift a Bud on occasion."

"Anheuser-Busch has spent considerable time looking at you and predicting your tastes. They're not blind to the fact that the category of specialty beers is growing by 20 percent annually. Like I said, quality not quantity. Like other boomers, you still have a taste for beer, but now you'll drink only one or two at a time. You're looking for quality, not quantity."

"Funny you should use that phrase. Hazen used it just the other night when he was talking about the boomers," I said.

"Not surprising," acknowledged Ruth. "Hazen and I talk a lot about this issue. But we're not the only ones. Marketers are very aware of this trend. Anheuser-Busch markets one of its brands, Michelob, into the boom generation. By associating it with golf and skiing—two high-end sports that boomers can afford—I guarantee that

Anheuser-Busch is counting on boomers to buy a few Michelobs. And just think a minute about all the 'boutique' beers popping up, with brew pubs at every ski hill. Samuel Adams is in the big leagues compared to some of the microbreweries attracting attention. Just recently *Boston* magazine included Tremont Ale in its 'Best of Boston' feature. After years as an on-tap product, this ale—made over in Charlestown—is now available in bottles. Just the fact that it is now being bottled shows how popular it has become," she said. "The shelves are getting more colorful every day with all the different labels sharing space."

"I never thought of it that way," I said. "And I never thought we'd be talking seriously about beer!"

"That's the point. We could be talking about any product. Look at the travel industry. Older Americans have higher household discretionary income per capita, fewer financial commitments, and more leisure time. Is it any surprise that, as the boomers age, the travel industry is booming? Just the other day I read that about five million vacationers were expected to book North American cruises in 1997. That's up from 4.65 million back in 1996. You can bet that the cruise lines are keeping a close eye on what the boomers want. But everybody can use this demographic information in their lives. You and Pieter can use it. Pieter can use it in his business. Both of you can use it to structure your financial affairs," she said.

"Now you're starting to sound like Hazen." We both smiled. "But it's funny you should mention that. Pieter and I have been talking about planning for the future.

CHAPTER SIX

It's so easy not to think about things. I mean, I feel bombarded by information—IRAs, 401(k)s, T-bonds, CDs. It's a real alphabet soup," I said.

"That's natural. Think about it for a minute. You and all the other boomers are just starting to think seriously about retirement. Given the size of your generation, that explains all the financial information that's hitting the market." Ruth stood up and stretched. "Meredith, would you mind walking down to the cafeteria with me? Dylan's still home and Hazen came over for dinner last night. Between the two of them, they kept me up till after midnight. I woke up late this morning and didn't have time to get a decent breakfast. I need a muffin. Let me treat you to one too."

"I'd like that," I replied, gathering my purse.

"Money. We're all preoccupied by it, aren't we?" said Ruth as she strode down the hall. I had to hustle to keep up with her. "We sometimes overlook the obvious, we're so obsessed by money. I have a wonderful uncle—a rabbi in New York—who's been a central influence in my life. He always used to say, 'Life is the greatest bargain. We get it for nothing.' I sometimes wonder if that explains why so many of us don't appreciate our lives. We didn't have to struggle to come by them and so we don't value them. Maybe that's why so many do nothing with their lives."

We arrived at the cafeteria and started moving through the line.

I said, "I think a lot of people in my generation have spent more time thinking about acquiring stuff than about how they're living their lives. Funny, I didn't real-

ize that until Pieter and I sold our house. It was a difficult decision. At the time, it felt like a gigantic step back-
wards. We just couldn't keep up with the rest of our
friends. But now I feel as if we'd been freed in a way. We
don't have to keep working for that house."

We both chose a banana muffin. Ruth took two coffee
cups and started filling them.

"It's so easy to get carried along by what everybody
else is doing," Ruth said. "All your friends have a big
house so you need one too. Before you know it, you're
not making your own decisions. Sometimes you need to
stand back and take a long, clear look at your own life
and see whether you're going down a path you like.
People are so afraid of changing their course and making
mistakes. Well, it's the people who make mistakes—who
go through difficult times—who end up happiest. And I'd
suggest that the people who are happiest have realized
that life's not a piece of cake. The happiest are those
who have found a way to deal with their problems. Hey,
I'm starting to sound like James Taylor."

We walked to the cashier and Ruth dug into her
pocket, pulling out a crumpled $5 bill.

"But for many baby boomers, life hasn't been all that
difficult," I said as we waited for the cashier to ring up
the sale. "I'd have to say my life was a breeze until
Pieter's business hit a bad patch and then we had to
start making some tough decisions."

"It sure does help to have a guide along the way, to
help you through those hard bits. I've been lucky. I've always had my uncle to turn to. He's now nearly ninety,
but I phone him every week just to check in, listen to his

advice. He spent a lot of time with me when I was young. He taught me about the value of meditation, the necessity of growing a soul. Funny—when you were talking about how we live our lives, it reminded me of something he would say. Much of life is beyond our control. We don't choose our families, our race. But the quality of our lives is ours to choose. We choose who to love, to befriend. We fashion our character, our spirituality. Uncle Jack would argue that we sacrifice our real wealth—the quality of our lives—in our unquenchable desire for material wealth—our things." We found seats outside overlooking the Charles River. We sat for a moment watching groups of students hustle back and forth to class, apparently happy and carefree.

"I didn't realize you were so religious," I said.

"I can't compare myself to my uncle. I do belong to a synagogue here, but my attendance isn't all that regular. I do, however, spend plenty of time thinking about and working on my spirituality. That's the thing about spirituality—because our lives are always in flux, because we are always growing and changing, we have to constantly reevaluate our spiritual needs. Let me give you an example. We use rituals to feed our spirits. You celebrate Christmas, right?"

I nodded. "It's my favorite holiday. I love the traditions—the baking, the caroling, the tree trimming."

"Have you changed those traditions over the years to include your kids?"

"Yes, of course," I replied. "We still celebrate with our families, but we have our own special time at home with only the four of us on Christmas morning."

"That's what I'm getting at. Our spiritual comfort depends to a large degree on where we are in our lives. Our lives are in flux. But for all that change, those rituals are actually a way of molding our lives around a constant set of values and a way of drawing connections with the past. We are not only individuals; we are part of a larger community."

"But how does all of this connect with choosing the quality of one's own life?" I asked.

"I firmly believe in the importance of creating one's own life plan. I agree completely with Hazen. Life is not a random walk. We should spend time predicting where we want to go, figuring out how to get there. For me, my spirituality has given me a framework—a set of moral obligations—that forms the basis of my life plan. And Uncle Jack always told me not to overlook the obligation to myself. That means taking responsibility for all aspects of my own life—social, intellectual, and financial."

"That sounds great, to go through life so sure of yourself. But things don't always work out as planned. Look at Pieter and me. Two years ago, I was certain I'd still be living out in the suburbs. Now I'm here, working with you. I could never have planned for that," I said.

"Unexpected things happen. It's how you handle them that's critical. I never expected to be where I am today. Having kids never crossed my mind. Then along came Dylan. My life was rocked to its core, but I handled it and Dylan has been the best thing that ever happened to me. Don't get me wrong. I'm not saying you should have a life plan that will tell you what you'll do and where you'll be on June 7, 2015. I'm saying that you should take a good hard look at your own life, figure out what you believe in, what you want to keep, what needs to be changed, where you want to go. If you've got that solidly in your head, when the unexpected happens then you'll be ready for it. You've got to build a lot of flexibility into your life plan because the unexpected will happen—and at the most inconvenient times. Dylan arrived the year I started teaching here. Just when I really wanted to focus on my career," she sighed. "Listen to me. I sound as if I've got life all figured out."

"Compared to most of the world, you do," I replied.

"No, I'm a firm believer that we've always got something new to learn. I see my life as a work-in-progress and I've never been afraid to accept advice. I've been lucky to have a wonderful guide in my life, but ultimately you have to develop your own vision of yourself. Your journey is your own and it continues until the day you die."

"I guess you're talking about developing a depth of character," I said.

"Exactly. And only you can be the author of your own character. Boy, this is a deep discussion for a Friday morning. Let's finish up and get started on our research work. This morning I want to teach you how to lead a discussion in a focus group. If we don't get at it, we'll be working until Saturday morning!"

⏤

After dinner, we let the kids off their dishwashing detail to watch a TV special. As they settled in for an evening of fine viewing, Pieter and I cleaned the table and loaded the dishwasher. We were in no hurry. Friday nights are always pretty low-key at our house; everybody's tired after a busy week.

"Ruth and I had quite a talk this morning," I told Pieter. "Actually, she did most of the talking. She treated me to a muffin and coffee and we ended up talking about the meaning of life."

"I thought she was a sociologist, not a philosopher," Pieter replied.

"Very funny," I said, cracking the tea towel on his backside. "It was quite illuminating. I think we've really got to think about the future—what we want for ourselves. She talked a lot about having a guide, about not being afraid to accept help from others. When I was coming home on the bus, I started thinking that we need a guide, a mentor. And guess who came to mind?"

"Hazen Armstrong."

"How did you know?"

"Because I've been thinking that we could learn a thing or two from him about planning our financial future," Pieter said.

"Hmm. Shall we talk to him tomorrow morning? He'll probably be out in the garden."

"Good idea. Now, enough serious talk. Let's get these dishes cleaned up."

7

Risk Nothing, Risk Everything

We woke up early on Saturday morning, as we always do. It's funny. When you're young, you can sleep in as long as you like. Then along come kids and you're up—early! The kids finally start sleeping in, but they've ruined you. Even though you desperately need the shut-eye, you'll never be able to sleep in again. Sleep, I'm convinced, is wasted on the young. But I was actually happy to wake up with the birds this morning. This was "P Day," the day we planned to search for a plan.

After a quick breakfast, Pieter and I left the kids fiddling around with the Internet—Malcolm was helping Emily gather information on box turtles for a school project—and we headed over to Hazen's. It was a beautiful spring day and, sure enough, Hazen was already puttering in his garden. It somehow seemed so right to be starting afresh—in the spring, in this garden.

"Good morning, you two. Isn't this just the best time of year?" Hazen said, gesturing toward the sun, still low on the horizon.

"We wanted to come over and tell you how much we enjoyed 'The World According to Hazen,'" I said as we passed through his gate.

"I was glad you could make it. You witnessed the introduction of my great new concept: passive predators. It came to me one day out of the blue."

"Don't laugh so fast. We've come to cash my first royalty check for providing you with that concept," I replied.

"What do you have in mind?" Hazen put down his shovel.

Pieter and I started to tell him how we had discussed some of the ideas he had mentioned and now wanted to put a financial plan in place. And we wanted his help. Hazen nodded, his smile indicating approval.

"That's great, but implementing a financial plan isn't something you do overnight," he explained. "You have to crawl before you run, and you have a lot of ground to cover before you'll have a solid financial plan in hand."

"You're right," said Pieter. "We are babes in the woods, but like any toddlers, we're curious and determined."

"Okay. The first step is the formation of your philosophy—the way you think about the investments you want or need to make. Follow me inside. I want to show you something that's helped me over the years. Maybe it'll help you too." He led us through his back door, pausing on the stoop to kick off his gardening boots, and we followed him through his kitchen and into his study. We walked over to a framed piece of calligraphy, a quote

94

from Shakespeare: "There is a tide in the affairs of men which, taken at the flood, leads on to fortune; omitted, all the voyage of their life is bound in shallows and in miseries. On such a full sea are we now afloat."

"It's from *Julius Caesar.* My mother trained as an artist, and this was one of her art school projects. She was always a great believer in taking charge of your own life," said Hazen, touching the corner of the frame. "It hung in the hall of our house forever. She gave it to me when I finished college way back when. It took on an added significance when I started my demographics work. The boomers became my tide. The boom is the full sea we're floating on."

Pieter had stood quietly, absorbing this bit of Shakespeare. "Yes, it makes good sense. This tells us to keep our antennae up, to be receptive to what's going on around us, to seize an opportunity when we see it. It's no coincidence that you're showing this to us," he said.

"No coincidence at all. You're right. Always keep your receiver switched on. When it comes to financial issues, the boom is sending signals that are loud and clear. You've only got to listen and then act on those signals."

"Enough already. Tell us what to do," I said.

"Nope. It's not that simple. I'm not responsible for creating your financial plan. You are. But I'm glad to point you in the right direction. How about this? Today I'll help you put together a list of what you should be thinking about including in your plan, plus I'll set you on your search· for a financial adviser who will help you manage your money. You can go off next week and do some preliminary groundwork. We can get together later in the week and review what you've accomplished. Then, over the next few weeks, I'll give you my views on the demographic trends affecting the real estate markets, interest rates, bonds, and stocks."

"But we thought you'd be our financial adviser," I said.

"No. I'd suggest you need professional, ongoing help. Look, if I was a doctor and you had a medical problem, you might ask me a few questions, but you'd still go to your own specialist. This is the same situation, only here we're talking about your financial rather than your medical health."

"But why can't we do the work we need by ourselves?" Pieter asked. "We're willing to do some reading. Why do we have to involve a financial adviser?"

"Good question. And once again, demographics and the boom gives us the answer. What did your parents do with their savings?"

"What little they did have they took to the bank and bought CDs or savings bonds," I said.

Pieter nodded. "My parents still do that."

"That's exactly the response I expected. For them the 1950s were easy. Easy jobs, easy promotions, then their homes took off in value in the 1980s. They left any savings they had at the bank and then your generation came along and bid up interest rates. Some of the smart ones in their generation invested, but not many compared to today. They were in the right place at the right time. Well, demographics tells us that's not an option for the two of you if you want to adequately provide for your retirement. The world's become a much more complicated place. And you're not going to be able to count on

Social Security to the same extent that your parents could," Hazen added. "By the way, plenty of boomers realize that they could use some help. According to a recent study I saw, nearly 75 percent feel they need guidance with their retirement planning. The number goes up to almost 90 percent for the generation behind the boomers. And they're right—they do need some help. *Money* magazine recently conducted a mutual fund IQ test. Less than 20 percent of respondents passed it. That's frightening considering that, in the last five years, about half of the nearly $1 trillion cash flow growth of the mutual fund industry came from a shift of household financial assets into equities. Most of the rest comes from money invested into 401(k) and IRA accounts. Do these people know what they're doing?"

"We're going to have to do things differently from our parents," I suggested.

"You're not only going to have to learn to save but you're also going to have to learn to invest. According to the old rule of thumb, if you saved 10 percent of your income, you were off to the races. That's not going to cut it any more. You not only need to save that 10 percent, but you also have to go out and find a good place to invest it, to get it earning the best return for you. And if you want to reap the best benefits, you won't be going down to the bank and plunking your money into CDs and savings bonds. You're going to have to get into the markets. You're going to need to educate yourself about money, and you're going to need help."

Striking a familiar note, Hazen continued, "Boomers are already making themselves felt in the markets. Like I mentioned earlier, the statistics show that in the past few years, Americans have already started investing a much larger percentage of their household wealth in the stock market—buying stocks directly and through mutual funds and retirement accounts, for example. The sheer number of boomers has complicated the investing field. Just look at the explosion that's hit the mutual fund industry. When they were your age, your parents probably never heard of mutual funds, and now you folks face a bewildering choice of thousands of funds. The fund-rating firm Morningstar tracks over 8,000 funds, helping consumers sort through them and chart their selections. And the array of products is only going to skyrocket even more. The investment industry is fully aware of your generation and the power with which you're going to hit the market—they want to cash in on you folks. That's going to bode very well for you. You'll have a tremendous number of products tailored to your specific needs.

"Now here's the downside. Do you have the time to make the best choice? I'd suggest that you're in the classic boomer trap. Both of you are working, your kids are still young, there aren't enough hours in the day. And you're not alone. Did you know that nearly half of all Americans consider themselves time-crunched? Not surprisingly, that number jumps to nearly 70 percent of all boomers. Of course, you're going to have to bone up on investing, do some reading. But do you really have the time to do the slogging it's going to take to keep on top of everything you'll need to know? Think back to buying your house. You probably invested quite a bit of your own time in the search. You probably got professional help too."

"Gee, we spent about six solid months looking for that house," I said, "scouring the newspapers and going out every weekend to model homes and open houses. Our real estate agent helped us out, and then we also used the services of a home inspector and an attorney."

"Okay. Saving for your retirement is every bit as important—probably even more so than buying a house. I'm expecting at least as much work on your part. You were willing to pay the real estate professionals for their services. I'm simply advocating that you'll need professional help with your investment decisions. But there's a bonus to this: studies show that investors with financial advisers typically earn higher returns than those who purchase investments directly. One recent study showed that, over a ten-year period, investors with professional help posted returns five times higher than those purchasing directly. Something else to consider: evidently, stock market investors without professional help are more likely to bail out of the market at the first sign of a downturn in the price of their stocks. An adviser provides a hand-holding service, reassuring investors that they won't lose their shirts and keeping skittish clients in the market, where they should be. A good adviser helps investors deal with the short-term emotions of fear and greed and focus on being patient— the one emotion that is the hallmark of a true long-term investor. It's a known fact that frequent trading will reduce your long-term returns. And that hand-holding service may have long-term benefits for the market as a whole. The vast number of boomers moving into the market is bound to bring more volatility—more players means more volatility, especially when many of these new players are not experienced in the ways of the market. But I'll get into that subject with you when we sit down to discuss the future of the stock market."

"Yes," Pieter said. "You make a strong case for getting professional advice, but who would we go to? Our retirement plan is with our bank. We'd have no idea whom to see."

Hazen smiled. "You're not alone. Lots of members of your generation are now looking for help. I was looking at some statistics which showed that back in 1991, only 38 percent of those aged forty-five to fifty-four were looking for retirement planning advice. By 1995, that number had jumped to 44 percent. People are getting wise to the fact that they could use professional help." Hazen looked at his watch. "It's getting on to ten o'clock. Why don't you two change into gardening clothes and I'll meet you back here in the garden? It's a particularly appropriate place to learn. We are going to 'grow' your knowledge—and I could use the help!" We all laughed. "The neighbors will think it's awfully kind of you to help out that poor eccentric guy across the street. Why not bring the kids? It's never too early for them to learn a thing or two about investing."

❧

We knew Hazen was having some fun with us, but this was too good to pass up. We returned home and collected the kids, who are always happy for the opportunity to muck about in the mud. The entire family was back at Hazen's in no time. Hazen brought out a tray laden with lemonade, tea, and cookies. We settled comfortably into lawn chairs and helped ourselves as Hazen instructed the kids to start digging up a bed at the foot of his backyard. Off they trotted with a shovel and a pitchfork. Interesting—the kids would have moaned and groaned about doing this work at home, but over at Hazen's it was fun.

"Okay," Hazen said, "where were we?"

"You were saying we weren't alone, that lots of boomers don't know about managing their money," I said.

"Let me expand on that a bit. A key part of managing your money is saving that money in the first place. You'll have nothing to manage if you don't save. Boomers, historically, have been spenders—big spenders. Consumers in the 1990s have more debts and use more credit than their parents did back in the 1960s. Did you know that interest payments for consumer credit—and that doesn't include mortgages—have become a larger portion of the household budget? Back in the 1970s, it took 200 percent of a young couple's income to buy a home. In the 1990s, that percentage had nearly doubled to almost 400 percent. Throw in another couple of tough stats—until very recently, many folks spent several years watching their real household incomes stagnate or head downward. It's no big surprise that personal bankruptcies rose by nearly 30 percent in the first four months of 1996.

"Despite today's good-news economy, I'd suggest that consumers are still feeling pretty beat up. Just making it from one day to the next has meant that the benefits of saving have been largely overlooked by boomers. Until now, that is. The economy's picked up, and this group is starting to mature, reaching a point in their lives where they have the money to save and can appreciate the benefits of providing for their future. Let me tell you what saving can do for you. Saving takes you out of living day to day. Too many of us live from paycheck to paycheck— even those who are in high enough income brackets to live otherwise. That approach to money saps all your energy and causes way too much family stress. You're caught in a vicious circle, never having enough money and always worrying about money. Planning for the future gives you confidence. A recent survey showed that people with a plan for their finances are more likely to believe that they will reach their goals in life."

"That's easy for you to say, Hazen," Pieter retorted, "but it's hard to save. We never have enough money to start to save, particularly this year."

Hazen nodded. "Yes, I know that's true. But even I can see how you two are handling your money problems in the short run. You're getting a grip on your finances. When you moved here, you had two vehicles. Now I see you're only operating the minivan. That's a good form of saving."

"You're right," Pieter said. "Once we got here, we saw we could make do with only one car. It took us a little while to get used to the logistics of not having two cars, but we figure we're saving a couple of thousand dollars each year."

"Then you're off to a fine start. You've made a wise short-term saving decision. It caused a bit of pain, but the benefits are clearly evident. Now let's tackle the long term. I'm going to start with plenty of questions. This will be your homework for the week. What are your debts, including personal loans and mortgages? How are you paying them back? Are you maximizing your contributions to your retirement plan? What does your asset mix look like? Is it right for you? How are you saving for your children's education? Do you have appropriate insurance coverage? Can you minimize your taxes?"

I took out a pencil and paper from my pocket. "Hold it, Hazen. Let me get it straight," I said, scribbling as if I was back in grade school.

"It's like a puzzle. Each of those pieces—repaying debts, saving, asset mix, insurance, taxes—not only fit together but they also affect one another. For example, the more you spend on insurance, the less you'll have available to save. The quicker you get your debts paid down, the quicker you'll add to your savings. It's all interrelated. There's one more thing I want to add to your homework. I'd like you to keep a running tally of how you're spending your money. Write it all down. If you buy a newspaper, jot it down. Books for the kids? Mark it down. This is a very good exercise. Not only does it tell you how much you're spending, but it will also highlight where you might cut back."

"Okay, so this is what we have to think about. But, Hazen, we're neophytes when it comes to this stuff," Pieter explained. I could hear the frustration in his voice.

"Hold your horses. You know me, I've still got lots left to say. First, however, I want to talk about the personal side of your financial plan. In order to set the parameters of your plan, you're going to have to ask yourselves some very personal questions. How committed are you to saving? You already know what it is to do without a second car. Savings comes at a cost. Maybe it's fewer restaurant meals, putting a few more miles on your old shoes before replacing them, bunking at a friend's cottage rather than taking an expensive vacation. What are you willing to pay to save? What is your risk tolerance?

"I mentioned the asset mix of your investments. Well, if you didn't believe in taking any risk, you'd turn to CDs. Historically, many Americans have been unwilling to take risks with their investments to earn a higher rate of return. Lucky for your parents, the economy complied and they could afford not to take any risk. You're not so lucky. You're going to have to turn to investment vehicles that are perceived to be riskier—like stocks—to adequately provide for your retirement. But remember, some parts of the stock market are riskier than others, so you're going to need to evaluate what kind of risk you two can live with."

"That's going to be a tough one. I'll admit I've always been sort of scared of the stock market," I said.

"You're not alone, Meredith. Let me ask you a question. Are you afraid of exercise?"

"I don't do it as often as I should, but that's laziness, not fear," I replied.

"Maybe you should be just a bit afraid of exercise," he countered. "Did you know that you'd be safer reading a book than running a mile? The act of exercising actually increases your risk of a medical problem—but only slightly. If, however, you survive your workout, you will have increased both your fitness and life expectancy. So, do the risks outweigh the benefits? The stock market presents the same dilemma. It does carry short-term risks. Yes, there will be corrections along the way when stock prices tumble. But holding sensible stocks—like sensible exercise—provides a terrific long-term benefit to your financial health.

"Here's another analogy, this time focusing on insurance. You always want to insure only what you *need* to insure. If you have a car, you need to insure it. If you have a young family, you need insurance, not only to protect your life but also to protect your income. What if you got sick and couldn't work anymore? That's a good argument for disability insurance. If you die, you need to know your family will be looked after. I must admit, I think the term 'life insurance' is a bit of a misnomer. If your car is stolen, you get a new car; but if you die, you certainly don't get a new life. What you're really insuring with life insurance is your income."

"You've given us some good pointers on our health and our insurance needs," I said. "In fact, we have been thinking about increasing our disability coverage. But, Hazen, how does this relate to investing in the stock market?"

"We've been talking about insuring your future. You may feel uneasy about stocks, but you need to purchase them to insure your income when you retire. You're focusing on only one risk: the ups and downs of the stock market. But you face other risks too. Don't underestimate how long you'll live. Plenty more folks in your generation will hit ninety than will get there in mine. By and large, you boomers are a healthy bunch. You risk running out of money long before you die. You have to plan to avoid that risk. I'd argue that this risk is exacerbated by the very size of your generation. The large number of boomers has put Social Security in jeopardy and, similarly, the size of your generation will contribute in large measure to keeping interest rates low for many years to come. The result? Low interest rates will mean that assets kept in fixed-interest-rate investments such as CDs can't grow fast enough to provide you with adequate funds for your retirement. There's risk no matter how you slice it, and I think you face a greater risk keeping your assets out of the stock market."

"I understand your argument, but I still feel I need to understand what we might be getting into," I replied.

"Good point, Meredith. I guarantee that the more you learn about the stock market, the more comfortable you'll be with it. First on the agenda, I'm going to send you down to the public library. Tell one of the reference librarians that you're putting together a financial plan and you'd like some basic information on plans and investing. Next, I want you to scour the newspapers for ads for seminars given by financial advisers. I want you to go to the first one you see—just to check it out. And I want you to take a look at the business pages of the newspaper every day. Read at least a couple of articles that concern investing. I'm going to go in and dig up a few of my favorite books for you to read."

As he walked into the house, I turned to Pieter. "Doing this right is going to take a lot of time."

"But Hazen made a good point. Look how much time and money we spent when we bought our house. Our financial plan deserves at least as much attention. Think about how we organized our IRA last year. We waited until the last minute and ran into the bank. A teller told us which mutual fund to buy. We did no research. If we told that story to Hazen, he'd have a fit!"

"I know you're right, but it's so much more fun going to open houses than trekking off to the library for investment books."

"Who knows, maybe we'll really get into it and start quoting the stock market pages to one another."

"Don't hold your breath, chum," I retorted. Pieter was much more analytical than I was. I had a sneaking suspicion that he was going to be the point man on this project.

The kids had finished their digging and had begun playing tag on the lawn. That quickly deteriorated into an exercise in futility for Emily; she could never catch her older, faster brother. After a heated shouting match, both kids came and sat with us, pooped from their morning's exertion. Hazen returned carrying five books.

"Here's your reading assignment. I picked these up at the Brookline Booksmith down on Harvard Street. First, *The Wealthy Barber* by David Chilton. You can't beat the basic information it provides about financial planning. And it's easy to read. It's told in a story format. Next is one aimed at folks your age. *Get a Financial Life* by Beth Kobliner. It concerns personal finance issues for people in their twenties and thirties. Another good basic book is *The First Book of Investing: The Absolute Beginner's*

Guide to Building Wealth Safely by Samuel Case. Here's one about investing in the stock market called *Learn to Earn*, by Peter Lynch and John Rothchild. Now, this one's for you, Meredith. It's called *The Beardstown Ladies' Common-Sense Investment Guide.* Actually, you'll like this one too, Pete. It's about a group of women who form an investment club—it has some great definitions and solid examples. These books cover a lot of the same territory we'll be going over in the next few weeks, but each one has its own spin on things, its own interpretation. I don't want you to think that this is the end of your reading. If you want to stay on top of this subject, it is absolutely essential that you keep reading. Gosh, I'm beginning to sound like my tenth grade economics teacher!"

"All these books remind me of that famous quote in the movie *Animal House*: 'Knowledge is good,'" Pieter quipped.

"I must have missed that one," Hazen muttered.

Pieter smiled. "It's a classic boomer movie. Since you study this generation, watching it should be your homework this week."

Hazen realized that Pieter was egging him on and continued with his financial lecture.

"Moving right along here . . . Now for the next chapter of the morning. As I said earlier, it's up to you to set the personal parameters of your financial plan. Once you've done that, I'd suggest you see a professional financial adviser to help you with the details of that plan. Take note, however: there's no point in using the services of an adviser unless you are prepared to organize your financial records and to commit to saving. You have to help yourself before you'll benefit from the help of an adviser. Courtesy of the boomers, there are now plenty around to choose from, all with different specialities. This is definitely a growth area—the number of people wanting to give you financial advice has exploded over the past few years. Some 25,000 entities are providing investment advice these days. And that's a good reason for you to be wary. There are some worrisome gaps in the regulation of this business. Buyer beware is the order of the day. Meredith, you might want to get your pencil and paper out again," he said, clearing his throat. I took his advice.

"Let's start with financial planners. These people will take a look at your overall needs, focusing on those areas that require attention. For example, I'd suggest that you probably need some help with your tax strategies. Meredith, have you given any consideration to how your new job will affect your tax situation? Do you know if you'll be able to write off a portion of your rent now that you're an independent contractor?"

"I hadn't even thought of that," I replied. "Would a financial planner help us with those sorts of issues?"

"Yes," answered Hazen. "Plus, planners will suggest money management strategies, where you can save and how to invest those savings. These people can also get into other territory. They'll give you advice on wills, powers of attorney, that sort of thing. They can handle all the basics. But, once again, beware. There are two types of financial planners: the fee-only and commissioned varieties."

"What's the difference?" asked Pieter.

"Fee-only planners charge you a set fee for establishing a plan. They usually bill on an hourly basis. You can expect to pay anywhere from $100 per hour on up. A basic financial plan takes approximately five hours to prepare. A critical question to ask is, 'How much will we have to pay for you to produce a plan?' Fee-only planners aren't selling a product, so the information they provide is considered independent thinking. After they give you the plan, they'll refer you to someone who can handle your specific financial needs.

"That's not the case with commissioned planners. These planners earn their income from commissions or fees they receive for selling their products to you, including life insurance and mutual funds. Unlike fee-only planners, they charge low fees or none at all." Hazen paused to pour himself another glass of lemonade.

"I get it," I said. "With a commissioned financial planner, they could be recommending a specific product and they'll be getting paid for that recommendation."

"Exactly," said Hazen, returning to his lawn chair. "There's nothing wrong with that, but you, the customer, should be aware of it. That means you should be asking a commission-based planner how they earn their compensation. Go into your dealings with open eyes. Shop around, ask questions, compare, get references."

"What about going to the bank? That's what we've always done in the past," said Pieter.

"And I bet your IRA is invested in your bank's own mutual funds, right?"

"Some of it is, but the rest is in a CD," Pieter answered.

"And do you use the services of the bank's private banker or do you just go to the teller for advice?" asked Hazen.

"So far, just the teller," said Pieter.

"Well, the banks have come a long way in the past few years," said Hazen. "They're aware of demographic trends too. They see increasingly savvy boomers who aren't content with putting their money in CDs. Nope, the old days are gone and the banks have seen the demographic writing on the wall. Most big financial institutions now offer their own line of mutual funds. Like commission-based financial planners, they'll be selling their own products. Plus they'll offer investment advice if you ask for it. These personal bankers usually limit their advice to the type of asset mix that's right for you."

"You mentioned that term 'asset mix' before. I'm not quite sure I know what you mean," I said.

"Generally, you build a portfolio of investment assets that reflects two things: your stage in life and your tolerance for risk. If you're retired, you'll allocate a larger portion of your investments to savings and income-producing investments. Why? Well, you'll need the income and you don't want to risk your security. But at your stage of life, you and Pieter should be more interested in investments with a solid potential for growth. That leads you—and the rest of the boomers—directly to the stock market. Of course, you'll still want a portion of your investments in savings, but nowhere near the amount you'd have in savings if you were retired. Advisers will use a formula to figure out what asset mix you should be striving for."

"It's amazing how everything takes us back to the baby boom," Pieter observed.

"Like I said, it's a powerful force in our economy. Now, back to financial advisers. You can buy your mutual funds from institutions like banks. But you can also deal directly with many of the mutual fund companies. This can be a good way to go if you know what you want to buy and you don't need much in the way of financial advice. But wherever you go to make your purchases, it pays to be a savvy consumer. There can be a variety of fees and expenses associated with these purchases. Administration, marketing, legal, and setup fees, for example.

"This is probably a good time to talk about loads. That's a fancy word for one-time fees paid when you buy or sell shares in a mutual fund. When it comes to loads, mutual funds break down into three types. You pay your fees right off the bat with front-end load funds. The fees could go as high as four or five percent. But, like I said earlier, it can pay to be savvy. This fee is usually negotiable with the adviser you're dealing with. Next are no-load funds. The name says it all—there's no charge to buy or sell these funds. And finally there are back-end or deferred-load funds. The fees become payable only at the time of sale. Often these fees decline over time. The longer you hold the fund, the less the fee when you go to sell—the reducing load acts as an incentive for you to hold onto the fund. Each of the three can have some advantages and some disadvantages. I know some experts think it's crazy to get into anything other than a no-load fund. That's certainly the opinion of Beth Kobliner,"

Hazen stated, picking up *Get a Financial Life* from the stack of books piled beside his lawn chair. "I think it depends on the individual funds. Once again, you should examine each fund on its own merits, and you have to ask questions."

"But what if we don't know what to buy? What if we need help?" asked Pieter.

"You might consider dealing with a brokerage firm. Brokers can sell a full range of investment products—everything from CDs to stocks, bonds, and mutual funds. Unlike bankers, brokers aren't tied to one line of products so they'll be able to offer you the full range of investment vehicles on the market. Expect to pay for these services, though. Brokers get paid for selling, earning commissions on the transactions they perform for their clients. As with other advisers, there's a range of fees. There are discount and full-service brokers. At a full-service broker—that's where you and your funds will receive the constant attention of your broker—expect to pay fees averaging about one percent of the value of your assets each year. Something called wrap-fee services are becoming increasingly popular, especially with the clients of larger brokerage firms. For investors who would prefer to pay one fee as opposed to costs based on each and every transaction, wrap-fee service is an ideal solution. Fees range from about 1 to 2.5 percent of the account—depending on the size of the account—and are charged on an annual basis. These services can be particularly well suited to a mature client who's accumulated a bit of wealth. I don't want to forget discount brokers. A discount brokerage usually charges one-third of what you'd pay at a full-service firm, but it's a question of getting what you pay for. Your money won't get the attention it would receive from a full-service broker."

"It boils down to figuring out the type of services and the level of attention we need. And personal attention comes with a price tag," I said.

"Partly right. But there's more," replied Hazen. "Choosing a financial adviser can be compared to selecting a doctor. You want somebody you like and, most important, you can trust. Ideally, you'll hook up with an adviser with whom you can develop a long-term relationship, someone who understands your needs, someone who's going to be around for a few years to tend to you. Remember, investing is a long-term process. It can take years to develop a portfolio that's just right for you. You don't want to be changing your adviser every year."

"So how do we find that person?" I asked.

Hazen chuckled. "Start shopping. I'd start by asking your friends for referrals. A word of caution. Be careful of choosing a financial adviser who's also a friend. Mixing friendship and business can cause problems. That's just one of the reasons I don't want to take on the role of your adviser. When you go to financial seminars, you'll see financial advisers strut their stuff; you'll hear them explain their approaches to investing. Of course, I'd always want to know what they think about the baby boom and demographics."

"Here we go. Back to the boom," I joked.

"We just can't avoid it," said Hazen, shrugging his shoulders. "I'd ask a few specific questions of the financial advisers. What's your training? What's your area of expertise? How are you paid? What about commissions? How often will you be in touch with me? How will you assess what I need? And don't get sucked in by the articulate incompetent."

"What on earth is an articulate incompetent?" asked Pieter.

"Beware people who sound great but don't ring true. Like I said earlier, the boom is putting pressure on the financial market, and there are lots of people now who want to help you with your finances. You need to take each sales pitch with a grain of salt. To do this, you have to build up your own knowledge base. And there's your start," said Hazen, pointing to our pile of books.

By this point, I was scribbling wildly.

"Meredith, you won't need to write this one down," said Hazen. "It's just common sense. Listen to yourself. Listen to your gut. Do you like the person? Remember, you're going to be telling this person your most intimate financial secrets."

I sat back in my lawn chair. "Whew. I think my hand's going to fall off. Thanks, Hazen. It all made good sense."

"Now the ball is in your court," said Hazen, collecting our lemonade glasses and teacups. "That's the end of today's sermon according to Hazen. We'll talk later in the week, but now I'm going back to my gardening." He walked over to the kids, who'd returned to digging in the backyard.

We watched Hazen talking to Malcolm and Emily.

"Well, we've talked the talk. Now it's time to plan the plan," quipped Pieter.

"Lame, very lame," I replied. "Let's just hope your research skills are better than your sense of humor."

8

That Sounds Like a Plan

Pieter and I were going to the movies Saturday night, but after our morning's discussion with Hazen, we revised our plans. Instead, we decided to stroll over to Bombay Bistro, our neighborhood Indian restaurant, a quiet place where we could talk and figure out how to tackle our financial plan. Our project seemed overwhelming to the two of us.

But as our dinner progressed, we made a good start, dividing up the chores into bite-sized pieces. We decided we'd both take a stab at reading the books Hazen had lent us. I assumed responsibility for phoning some of our friends to check out whether they used the services of a financial adviser and, if so, who and why. We brought along a copy of Saturday's newspaper, and a quick skim of the business section revealed two financial seminars that we could attend in the next couple of weeks. Pieter planned on visiting the library to pick up some more goodies. I would phone our bank to arrange a meeting with a private banker. Pieter decided to surf the Internet to see what types of financial information he might find there.

We even carved out the time to do all these errands. We both decided to scrap our lunch hours, pack bag lunches instead, and pursue our hunt for financial information. By the time coffee and dessert arrived, the whole exercise didn't seem nearly as daunting. And the restaurant meal was the first entry in our book recording how we were spending our money. Hazen would be proud. Heck, we were proud of ourselves.

Pieter took Malcolm and Emily to the library Sunday afternoon. The kids were looking for more stuff on box turtles, and Pieter planned to buttonhole a librarian for some information on financial matters. I spent the afternoon on the phone with a few friends.

My first call was to our old next-door neighbors in the suburbs. Tom and Heather are both attorneys who, like us, had been going through some tough times. Heather had bowed out of the work force a couple of years ago when she gave birth to their fourth child. Tom's firm had just disbanded and he'd struck out on his own, setting up an office by himself. Heather told me they'd been using the services of a full-service brokerage firm for the past ten years. Neither of them had a pension, she explained, so they knew they'd be relying on their retirement accounts and other savings to fund their retirement years.

"We know that we don't have either the time or expertise to manage our investments," she confessed. "Using a broker has made our lives a lot easier. Our broker got us into a regular monthly system of contributing to our retirement plans. It's funny—if you don't actually see the money in your hands, it's a lot easier to save it. Plus, we don't leave everything until the last minute like we used to. Despite the financial ups and downs we've had over the past few years, our savings are well into six figures.

"But saving for the kids' education has sucked up a lot of our investment dollars," she continued. "With four kids, it's a big concern. It costs well over $10,000 each year just in tuition fees alone—and that's in today's dollars. We estimate it's going to easily cost double that by the time it's the baby's turn to head off, what with government cutbacks, inflation, and economic pressures on the budgets of universities and colleges. And that's without factoring in the cost of housing, books, and clothing. No one has the magic number, but rest assured, it's going to be big. And let's face it, if our kids are going to have a chance of success in this world of rapid change, they need to be educated."

In an effort to prepare for the future, Heather told me that they had set up trust accounts in the names of each of their children. Heather admitted that they were lucky. When each child was born, her parents had given a gift of $5,000. "That was a nice start, but we're very consistent about depositing Christmas and birthday money gifts," she explained. They had invested in equity mutual funds (funds invested in the stock market), avoiding the kinds of funds that paid out interest or dividends because that money could be added to Heather and Tom's income and taxed in their hands. This way, the gains the equity fund made over the long run would be added to their kids' incomes and, as a result, taxed at a much lower rate because they would be in the hands of their children. I tacked one more thing on our financial housecleaning list: Move Emily and Malcolm's money out of T-bonds—pronto!

Heather also told me that a few years back, she and Tom visited an accountant to structure their tax issues. She suggested that this might be a good idea for me, now that I was working from the house.

Next, I phoned Rick and Margo, the parents of Malcolm's best friend. I had always been impressed by their frugality. Younger than Pieter and me, they own their home mortgage-free. Margo teaches school and Rick is a social worker at a local group home. Rick answered the phone. I had inadvertently struck a gold mine. I hadn't realized that saving and investing is Rick's passion and hobby. A self-professed do-it-yourselfer, Rick told me he spends anywhere from ten to twenty hours a week tending to the family's savings and investments.

"I love it. I should have become a financial planner, and who knows, with the way governments are now, I might be looking for a new job soon," he said with a laugh. He suggested that Pieter and I take a look at two magazines—*Kiplinger's Personal Finance Magazine* and *Money*—for tips on insurance, tax issues, and investing matters. He told me that he got started on his "hobby" out of fear of financial disaster.

"About ten years ago, I realized we were spending far more than we were earning, and if we didn't get it under control, we were headed straight for bankruptcy proceedings. It was the credit cards that were really killing us. Of course, we weren't alone on that one. Did you know that consumers have charged nearly $400 billion in credit card debt? Pretty scary stuff. Margo went back to teaching and that saved us. Plus, we spent every spare penny paying off our debts—not on acquiring more things. Otherwise, we'd be just one more statistic, part of the downward trend of the shrinking middle class in this country." I was surprised not only by his frank recollections but how the two of them had put themselves back on track. There was definitely hope for us.

"You realize that you're going to need to build up a pretty big nest egg if you want to retire comfortably?" Rick asked. He continued telling me that we should aim for a retirement income of 70 percent of our final preretirement salary. Historically, retirees have relied on the "three-legged stool" of retirement income—government pensions, employer-sponsored pensions, and personal savings. "I see our generation looking at a two-legged stool. I'm not counting on Social Security," he said. "Margo and I currently have a combined salary of $65,000 a year. We're aiming to have retirement income of about $50,000 per annum. Remember, we both have pension plans. But we figure we'll need at least $500,000 by age sixty-five to maintain our current standard of living. You and Pieter will need even more because I suspect that neither of you is entitled to an employer-sponsored pension. I know this is going to shock you, but the two of you will need $1 million by age sixty-five. It sounds like a lot—and it is—but if you get an early start, you can make it.

"I know you and Pieter are computer literate," he added. "There are several good software programs to calculate the retirement income you'll need and how much you'll have to put away to generate that amount. Why don't you take a look at *Quicken Financial Planner?* It gives good all-round tips on financial and retirement planning. It also provides Morningstar reports on mutual funds. Financial advice is built into the program as well."

I remembered Hazen mentioning Morningstar and decided to mark down the name of the software. I then asked him if he had ever used the Internet as a resource tool.

"All the time," he answered, telling me that many of the major financial institutions have home pages describing their services. In addition, the Net offered plenty of other investing information. "You can contact everybody from money managers to colleges to stock markets from around the world on the Web. The *Quicken* software is good for that too—it provides links to Net resources. I saw a home page for the Zagreb stock exchange the other day." He laughed. "But you know, it saves hiking all over town and making dozens of phone calls." He suggested we search the Web—not only under the names of the specific companies and issues that interested us, but also under more general headings such as "personal finance and investment."

"But what if we don't have the kind of time you spend on investing?" I asked.

"I have just the person for you," Rick replied. "My cousin is a financial planner. Actually, she sends me a lot of material on mutual funds. Plus, she's a good source of advice on all the recent changes to IRAs, capital gains, and estate taxes. She charges a fee to draw up a financial plan, but if you decide to have her implement the plan for you, she will often waive the fee." I thought back to what Hazen had told us about financial planners. Rick's cousin seemed to be a hybrid of a fee-only and commission-based planner. Definitely worth a call.

"One final word of advice," Rick said. "Whatever you do, don't be too conservative in your planning and investing. There are several items that people don't think enough about." He listed three topics—inflation, life spans, and overly conservative investment strategies. The effects of inflation, he explained, are easy to overlook when it's hovering around 2 percent. But inflation has a cumulative effect, reducing spending power by approximately 30 percent over the years that our generation will be accumulating its retirement nest egg.

"Here's the good news," said Rick. "You and Pete will probably live longer than you think. Most of us think we'll have only ten years of retirement before we check into the Great Beyond. In fact, the average person can expect nearly twenty years of retirement. Here's the bad news. Many folks aren't saving enough for all those extra years.

"I'd suggest that many boomers are currently investing their retirement dollars too conservatively," he continued. "All the statistics suggest that a well-diversified portfolio will always outperform simple bank deposits. 'Be an owner, not just a loaner.'"

Finally, I phoned Nathalie, an old high-school friend of mine. She's divorced, has no kids, and is a nursing administrator at a local hospital. I'd always admired her investing savvy. She owns a couple of houses in our neighborhood that she rents out to college students.

"How odd that you should be phoning me," she said when I told her the purpose of my call. "I'm just in the process of reevaluating my investments. I'm contemplating diversifying my holdings. I know I'm too concentrated in one area, and real estate has had its ups and downs recently. But I'm not sure where to go to next." I ended up telling her about Hazen, the boom, and the stock market. We agreed that I'd pass along my tips to her.

Just as I was saying goodbye to Nathalie, I heard the kids and Pieter coming in the front door.

"Hey, Mom," called Emily from the front hall. "Do you want to see how a box turtle lays its eggs? It's really cool and gross."

By the time I walked into the hall, Emily was well into unpacking her backpack, digging around for that cool, gross picture. Pieter had his hands full of books too.

"Here. Let me take those," I said. "So how did it go?"

"A big success. But we've got a lot of reading ahead of us. The reference librarian showed me all sorts of stuff. There are plenty of newsletters kept in the reference section. They contain up-to-the-minute information on investing and details about share prices and activities of companies. They've also got a database that lets you call up investing information. And there's a huge collection of personal finance magazines. I brought this one home," he said, holding up a copy of *Money*.

"It has an article about demographics and investing," he said, searching through the magazine. "Here it is. 'Ride the Echo Boom to Stock Market Profits.' It's all about the kids of the boomers—they're called the echo boomers, and there are some 76 million of them under twenty—and the impact their spending power gives them. It says here that eight- to seventeen-year-olds in America have a personal income from gifts, allowances, and part-time jobs that is almost as large as Ireland's gross domestic product. Companies like Nike, Gap, Mattel, and Disney are poised to collect from these young consumers, so it could pay off to invest in these companies now. Looks like Hazen's not the only one to be tuned into the power of demographics."

"I had a fruitful afternoon too," I said. "Not only did I come up with a couple of names of people we should contact, but I also scored two invitations to dinner. But you know the most interesting thing? Our friends are all concerned about their financial futures. They're all thinking about how to fund their retirements. Hazen and Ruth are right. The boom is growing up."

"Mom, I found it!" shouted Emily. "Here it is," she said, sticking the book under my nose.

"Yep. That's gross," I acknowledged. Box turtles took over from boomers and their finances as the topic-of-the-minute in the DeMarco household.

—

After dinner, the kids sat down to watch *The Simpsons*, our Sunday-evening tradition. Pieter headed downstairs to our computer. Over dinner, I had told him about Rick's comments about the Net.

"Meredith. Hey, Meredith! Come on down here for a minute."

I descended to the basement to find Pieter sitting before the glowing screen.

"Rick was right. You can't believe what a find this is. Look at this," he said. "Here's a list of sites on learning to invest, another on mutual funds, information on stocks and bonds. I've watched TV commercials advertising these sites but I never thought there would be so much information on them. Here's something on the screen called Money Online—it's related to *Money* magazine. And I marked another couple of sites down. One is called AAII On-Line—it's the home page of the American Association of Individual Investors and it's full of articles. Another interesting one is Financenter. It gives interactive calculations and statistics and also is a way to hook up with insurance companies and mortgage lenders, for example. I'm going to give old Hazen a call. I bet he doesn't know about this stuff," he said, reaching for the phone.

"Hi, Hazen. Pieter here. I'm sitting at my computer and you should see what I've discovered," he said. He paused, listening. "So you already knew all about this stuff. You just wanted to see whether I was keen enough to find it myself. Well, aren't you the sly dog." Pieter laughed, turning to me and rolling his eyes heavenward. After a few moments of chatting, he hung up.

"He says he's so impressed with our resourcefulness that he'd like to invite us on the Hazen Armstrong Real Estate Tour next Sunday morning. As a bonus, he'd like to take us out for brunch after the tour."

"Sounds lovely," I said. "That was worth the trip downstairs. Now I'm going back to see what's happening in Springfield." I leaned over and kissed the top of Pieter's head. Things were definitely starting to get fixed in this house.

9

Out from Under

"I had my own little focus group going yesterday," I chirped as I walked into Ruth's office Monday morning. We were scheduled to spend a couple of hours fine-tuning the discussion guide I would be using to lead the boomer focus groups.

Ruth looked up from her computer keyboard. "You're bright and chipper today."

"Pieter and I had a very productive weekend. We've decided to get our financial house in order. Hazen set us on a course of collecting financial information, and yesterday I phoned around to a few of my boomer friends to see what they're doing for retirement planning. Although it was a rather small poll, I think you'll be interested in the results."

"Do tell."

"It seems boomers are coming of age. Contrary to what the popular press says, many are busy saving and investing. They're taking different approaches, but they're concerned about providing for their kids' educations and their own retirement," I explained.

"I'm not at all surprised," Ruth said. "The media love bad news. Telling the boomers that they will never be able to save enough for their retirement is a great scare story. The media thrive on tension and create it by exploiting the boomers' natural pessimism about the future."

"What do you mean, natural pessimism? I've always thought of myself as an optimist," I said. "That's the thing that bugs me about talking about boomers: we all get lumped together as if we all think and do the same things. Look, even I'm guilty of that."

"I'm talking about your generation as a whole," Ruth replied. "Collectively, your generation was born with a gigantic silver spoon in its mouth. Boomers won the big prize simply by being born on this side of the Atlantic— much better than arriving in a bombed-out European city. In the 1950s and 1960s, real incomes were steadily increasing, our economy was hopping, and your parents could afford to give you nearly everything, including a great education. Boomers are the best-educated genera-tion in the history of the world."

"Sounds great so far. When does the pessimism come into the picture?"

"Think about it. Boomers grew up thinking the world was their oyster. It's been called the psychology of enti-tlement. They were entitled to feast on that oyster. Over their lifetimes, the boomers have faced huge pressures to consume. Advertisers bombard us, telling us our lives are not complete without a new car, a new refrigerator, a new lawnmower, a new computer. Boomers grew up be-lieving they are entitled to those goodies. 'You deserve a break today,' according to the McDonald's jingle. 'Just do it,' Nike tells us. But it hasn't worked out that way. Boomers aren't entitled to the good life simply because of when they were born. They can't do whatever they want, whenever they want. When they started to learn that they didn't automatically inherit the good life, that they were going to have to go out and earn it, the pessimism started to creep in to the picture. I'd argue that the pessimism has increased as boomers have learned that they are going to have to work even harder than their parents did to earn the good life."

"But how did that happen? How did things get so difficult?" I asked.

"It's a combination of things. First, we tend to forget that the 1950s were an aberration. In its history, the world has rarely seen such a long run of stability and good fortune. Generations that came before yours had a good understanding that life was going to be tough. Boomers didn't have to learn that hard lesson until relatively late in life. Second, the boom is its own worst enemy. Here's a huge group of people competing for jobs, positions, money. It's sort of like a game of musical chairs. More than a few of you are going to end up losing out, experiencing a huge gap between your aspirations and your opportunities. Third, we're living in a world of enormous social and technological change. Think of how many of your friends are divorced, living alone, or far away from their hometowns. We don't have the comforting and comfortable established routines that our parents did. Yes, we are free of the hidebound traditions of the 1950s, but as more than one commentator has written, with freedom comes anxiety. Fourth, when you grow up thinking you're entitled to the good life, you're bound to be disappointed by what fate has in store for you."

"I'd certainly agree with you that we've had to work harder than our parents to make ends meet. That's been tough to cope with."

"Since the late-1980s," Ruth said, "incomes have been stagnant for many families in this country. Boomers had no clue that anything like this was even possible, and it's hit them like a ton of bricks. For years, they'd watched their incomes march ever upwards. Not a pretty picture for a group of people who believe they're entitled to consume, consume, consume."

"So how are we ever going to save for our retirement?" I asked.

"Well, I'm too old to be a boomer, so I can be optimistic," laughed Ruth. "And I think the signs, so far, are very promising."

"Do tell," I said, mimicking her.

"We're constantly deluged by magazine and newspaper articles telling us boomers are not good savers, they rack up huge credit card debts and are completely unable to control their urge to consume. There have even been calls for legislation to expand pension coverage to address the problem of boomers' inability to save. But there are plenty of signs to the contrary, indicating that boomers will be able to save for their retirements." Ruth rose from her chair and began searching through a pile of papers.

"I'd agree with that. Look at our friends. They've all begun saving," I said.

"Here, I found it," she said, pulling a couple of articles from a file folder. "Plenty of statistics show that boomers are beginning to put themselves on an economic diet. Here, look at this article from a magazine called *American Demographics*. During the recent economic slowdown, consumers were willing and able to cut down on their spending. During the 1980s—when the economy was recovering from a brutal recession but the boomers were younger—consumer spending continued to grow at rates ranging from 4 to 5 percent each year. But this time around, as we've pulled ourselves out of another harsh recession, consumer spending has only been growing by about 2 or 3 percent a year. But here's something interesting from *Fortune* magazine. Over the past decade, the portion of Americans who own stocks has nearly doubled to approximately 40 percent. And the mutual fund industry has been the happy recipient of a significant portion of that increase. During the same time period, assets of the mutual fund industry have expanded at a 16 percent rate."

"I can believe that. Look at all those mutual fund ads you see on the TV these days," I said.

"That's telling us something. As boomers mature, they're learning that they're going to have to look after themselves. They're also learning that they can economize if they must. It's like my uncle always used to say: 'You can't sit on two horses with one behind.' Another of his Yiddish proverbs. It seems that boomers are beginning to grasp that concept. Maybe we don't need quite so much stuff as we've been led to believe."

"That's a lesson we've learned over the past year—you can do just as well with less. It actually feels good to be out from under all the burdens that buying so much stuff puts on you. That saying of your uncle's reminds me of a story that's had a huge influence in my own life. I have a friend whose mother won the lottery—a million bucks. My friend grew up in pretty humble circumstances and her mother's weekly splurge was a tin of salmon. When she won the lottery, her kids would tease her that she could go out and buy all the tins of salmon she wanted. Her mother always replied, 'Sure, but I can still only eat them one at a time.' Maybe we don't need as much stuff as we have stockpiled in our houses. Like you say, one behind, one horse."

"Here's another point. Boomers are getting a bad rap." Ruth pulled out another article. "This study shows that Americans between the ages of 35 and 54 began saving for retirement at a median age of 30, but people who are now 55 and older began saving at a median age of 42. Here's some equally interesting data, arguing that it's not until people are in their forties and fifties that they really start saving. Before that they're too busy spending, starting up their homes and raising children. And it's not until they've reached late middle age that their incomes peak. The baby boom is just reaching those age groups. Now we'll see savings start in earnest in this country."

She picked up a third paper. "Here's more support for that—a report on mutual fund ownership. The vast majority of fund shareholders—a whopping 84 percent—are saving primarily for retirement. The typical mutual fund shareholder is forty-four; and, not surprisingly, as house-hold income rises, so does mutual fund ownership, par-ticularly ownership in equity funds. People start saving more as they age. Not only are they more concerned about providing for their retirement, but they also have more money to save. Generally, the higher the age, the lower the financial obligations—children are raised, houses are paid for. Plus, the higher the age, the higher the real income. What we're going to see in the next decade is a huge group of boomers moving into their prime years for saving. And I know that as I got older—or should I say matured—the issue of retirement started to edge into my mind. I worried about it, and I certainly pay a lot more attention to my pension and my other in-vestments than I did ten years ago."

"Let me get this straight," I said. "You're suggesting that many boomers haven't yet hit the years where they really get into saving."

"Exactly. Here's another interesting point. Once they get into saving, people stay in that mode for a good long time. Economists talk about the savings profile of indi-viduals. On a graph, it looks like a big hump. We save very little when we're young. In fact, we're busy borrow-ing to finance our education and our house. Inter-estingly, the generation behind the boomers is proving to be very concerned about saving for retirement—76 percent of those aged eighteen to thirty say saving for re-tirement is their primary reason for investing. But it's not until late middle age that we reach the peak of our savings years. Then, as we move into old age, we 'dis-save'—that's when we start spending our savings during our retirement years. I think that boomers are going dis-save at a later age than today's retirees."

"Why?" I asked.

"Early retirement is a hot issue right now—partly be-cause of the boomers. The boom is placing pressure on older workers to retire in order to make room for the boomers nipping at their heels. When your generation hits retirement age, the demographic structure of the workforce is going to be quite different than it is today. In twenty years, there will be no new boom pressuring older workers—namely the boomers—to leave their jobs. That's because the generation behind the boom is about 30 percent smaller. That's why I'd estimate that, in the next couple of decades, individual seniors will start dis-saving at an even older age than they are now."

"Interesting. But there's one thing that bothers me about your analysis. In every discussion of the baby boomers, all boomers are lumped together as if we all do exactly the same thing at the same time, think the same way, eat the same things, buy the same stuff. It drives me crazy," I said, shaking my fist.

"Spoken like a true boomer. You folks all sound the same."

"Stop it. Stop it right now. I know you're trying to give me a hard time." By now we were both laughing.

"No, I mean it. 'Everybody looked the same, everybody acted the same, and everybody wanted to be the same.' Do you know who wrote that?" Ruth asked.

"Let me guess. Hazen Armstrong?"

She gave a shriek of laughter. "Close, but no cigar. That was Pete Townshend of The Who. He also wrote, 'I hope I die before I get old.' I wonder if he still feels that way. By the way, rock 'n' roll has been one of the key things tying all you characters together. Boomers have always wanted to be seen as individuals. That's why you sound like a true boomer when you take affront at me lumping you all together. But here's the deal. People growing up together absorb and are affected by the same issues and events."

"Yes, but people can experience the same event and have a very different take on things," I replied.

"True enough. But there's more. There are certain fundamentals that everyone, regardless of when he or she was born, experiences. We all have to find a job, house ourselves, feed ourselves, entertain ourselves. And even if individuals think differently, there are many in society who have made and will continue making them function like a homogeneous group. Think about how many articles you see these days bemoaning the fact that boomers are spoiled brats, forever demanding more and more and more. Generation Xers, those born at the tail end of the boom, like to slag the entire group of boomers too. The other day, I saw an article entitled 'The Case for Boomer Euthanasia' in a local Gen X newspaper. And don't forget the profit angle. The commercial impact of the generation has been mined along the way, with corporations tapping into the boom generation at every stage of its development. First it was baby food, then blue jeans, fast food, minivans; now it's computers. Did you know that, since the early-1980s, the number of households owning home computers has increased fivefold? Bill Gates has boomers to thank for that phenomenal growth. By specifically targeting this generation, marketers have made the boom generation more aware of itself and its influence, thus making it even easier to market to them—a very fruitful loop, I might add," Ruth concluded with a flourish.

Ruth and Hazen certainly shared plenty of ideas. "So it's just marketing that makes us think we hang together as a group?"

"No. There's more to it than that. Boomers are still going through experiences en masse—experiences that continue to define the generation," Ruth said.

"Like what?" I asked.

"The time crunch is a good example. More women than ever are working outside the home, and boomers are living increasingly harried lives as a result. More than half of all boomers are stressed out by juggling jobs, parenting, and trying to squeeze in a personal life. And women are more time-stressed than men. Did you know that a recent survey of working adults revealed that, given the choice, 51 percent of them would pick more time over money? The time pressure cooker has become a universal boomer experience."

"You're so right. The kids tell me that I usually sound like the White Rabbit. I'm late, I'm late, for a very important date."

Ruth laughed. "Listen, we're going to be late with this discussion guide if we don't get at it."

"Right. And I'm not going to have any money to save unless we get to work," I replied.

We got down to business.

10

The Real
Real Estate

"I hope you're wearing comfortable shoes," said Hazen as he opened the door to welcome us on Sunday morning.

"You better believe it. It's a glorious spring day," said Pieter. "What could be better than learning about finances and getting a bit of exercise all at the same time?"

"Spoken like a true boomer, Pieter. Why only do one thing when you can save time by doing two?" Hazen quipped. "Shall we head off on our real estate lecture now? We can stop along the way for refreshments. Our first stop isn't far away," he said, locking the front door behind him. "Hold it right there," he shouted at Pieter and me as we reached the end of his walkway. "This is where my lecture begins—at my own house."

"Hey, I thought we were going for a real walk," I said.

"All in good time. We have lots of real estate yet to see, Meredith, but first I want to talk about this particular piece of residential real estate." We turned to stare at Hazen's house, a sturdy three-story red-brick edifice set on a small, narrow downtown lot. Unlike many of the houses along the street, it did not sport a rear addition or skylights. Hazen had kept it up very well, however; the shingles looked almost new, the white enamel trim sparkled in the morning sunlight.

"This house was built in the 1930s. I bought it back in 1967 for $35,000 when I moved to Brookline. I had inherited some cash from my grandmother and this was my first investment in the real estate market. That was a fairly high price for this neighborhood at that time, but it was in excellent condition and I liked the house. It reminded me of the home my grandmother had lived in. See, even I can get emotional about my investments. To be honest, apart from regular maintenance, I really haven't changed too much over the years. I watched its price rise at a slow but steady rate of about 10 percent a year through the '60s and '70s. There were some years when there was no appreciation, and others when I made more than 10 percent. Then along came the '70s and '80s; the huge increase in interest rates—to the 18 to 19 percent range—meant that value went down. But by the mid-'80s, things really started to cook, and growth lasted until 1988. In the early '90s, there was a devastating bust, but since 1996 things have been steadily improving. Real estate experts are predicting a more controlled boom, with buyers being a lot more cautious. It's probably worth about $355,000 today."

"And you're going to blame this on the baby boom, right?" joked Pieter.

"You got it," Hazen laughed. "Housing is a commodity. Why should the boom's effect on real estate be different from its effect on any other commodity? But there are many other real estate markets in this country besides the residential market in Massachusetts, and the pressure the baby boom brings has had a different impact on each of them. That's what this Sunday morning tour is all about. I'm going to show you that the real estate market is no longer one monolithic elephant. Your parents were lucky. They could have put their dollars into virtually any real estate market in this country and turned a tidy profit. When your parents bought their homes, the real estate market was in a state of equilibrium—a more or less equal number of buyers and sellers—and it had been that way for years. Then along came the boom and threw the market into disequilibrium with many more buyers than sellers. And you know what that does to prices.

"These days, I'd liken the real estate market to a stock market. You have to know where to invest and you have to know how to play the market to your personal advantage. Critical to knowing where to invest is understanding the demographics at play in the market. Think really long term. There's going to be a point in a couple of decades when the boom begins leaving the real estate market—selling the family home. What do you think will happen to residential real estate prices then? Who are you going to sell your house to? Here, let's walk down the street a bit."

We ankled down the sidewalk, admiring the freshly planted gardens.

"Stop here," Hazen instructed. We found ourselves in front of a house similar in size to Hazen's but slightly more gussied up—a new front porch, new windows all around. "The history of this house is a perfect example of the power of the boom. When I moved into this neighborhood, an elderly couple lived in this house. They'd raised their kids here. The husband died and the wife sold the place back in 1983. A couple in their mid-thirties bought it for $215,000. They did all these renovations and put the place up for sale in 1986. I think they were transferred to another city. Their timing was perfect. Another young couple in their mid-thirties paid top dollar. According to the real estate agent, it sold for $420,000 in 1986, and it's not all that much different from my place. Today, it'd be worth about $350,000. The question is, who's going to buy this place next and what's it going to be worth?"

"This is a such a pretty house," I said. "And it's in a good neighborhood. They shouldn't have too much trouble selling it."

"That's the traditional view of real estate in this country— a nice house in a good neighborhood will sell for a tidy profit. But that's Peter Pan thinking. It's time to grow up, freshen up our view, and put a demographic spin on things. The oldest baby boomers—the first cohort— started to enter the housing market in the late 1970s. The rest of the gang joined in during the 1980s. If you recall, the country was in the midst of a recession then and enduring sky-high interest rates. As a result, many of those boomers started off renting, delaying the purchase of their first home. When the economy recovered in the mid-1980s, they flocked into the housing market. That's what happened to this place," said Hazen, gesturing at the house.

"And that explains the skyrocketing prices," said Pieter.

"Right. Supply and demand. The construction industry kicked into high gear, building suburban homes on the periphery of American cities. And the younger boomers—the second cohort, the largest of the two boomer groups—ended up paying top dollar for their real estate because the prices were driven up by their older brothers and sisters. So where does this leave us?" he asked.

Pieter turned to him. "Well, using your supply-and-demand logic, now that the youngest boomers are housed, there will likely be an oversupply of houses in the future and prices will go lower than before—not overnight, of course, but there will be a gradual decline over the next twenty to thirty years."

"That's a good start. You're picking this stuff up. Remember those weekends when suburban model homes were inundated with boomer buyers? That's not happening anymore, and we're watching those real estate developers filing for bankruptcy. The construction industry didn't understand the demographics at play, in combination with a tough economy, and they overbuilt, leaving lots of unsold new housing stock—starter homes in particular—sitting out there in the suburbs for a good long time. There were very few buyers coming along to absorb that oversupply. The boom skewed their view.

Historically, the real estate market has seen five- to seven-year cycles. Because of the boom, the cycles are completely thrown off for the next twenty years, I'd estimate," said Hazen.

"So what does the future hold?" I asked.

"Even though the housing market has been hot in recent months, I'd say that has more to do with pent-up demand rather than being a new, long-lasting boom. Long-term demand is definitely waning for residential properties. The number of first-time home buyers is declining. These are people aged twenty-five to thirty-four, and this group is going to decline in size from its current number by about 10 percent by the end of this decade. Add to this numerical decline a 'social' decline in the demand for first-time homes. The Generation X group doesn't seem as quick to leave the nest as the older baby boomers. And it seems that those in their twenties, the baby busters, are choosing to live with their parents or roommates a little longer. Structural changes in the economy—some caused by the boom itself—are often blamed for retarding job entry for Gen Xers and baby busters. And that's bad for real estate. The percentage of people who are forming new households is in a decline. So here's the bottom line: housing prices are unlikely to return to the big prices of the 1980s. Let's take a look farther afield," said Hazen, leading us to the Brookline Village "T" station. After a quick train ride downtown, we were soon strolling along the Charles River, with the dome of MIT providing a picturesque backdrop across the water.

"But you're only talking about first-time buyers," Pieter said as we dodged the rollerbladers and cyclists along the path. "Think of all the boomers who are moving up to their second and third homes. Isn't that going to push up demand?"

"I don't know about that. You are right, there will always be people who want the bigger and better house and who can afford it, so we might see some movement in higher-priced homes. That ties in perfectly, likening the real estate market to a stock market. Higher-priced homes could be a niche market. But don't forget that an important part of trading up is selling your own home—and that could be difficult. Plus, many boomers bought their homes for more than they can sell them for in today's market. That leaves them at a disadvantage when it comes to trading up. There are a few other items to factor into the mix. Boomers had their children at an older age than their parents and now they have to think about providing them with college educations. That may divert money that would otherwise be spent on trading up to a more opulent home. And I just wonder whether more than a few people are stopping to think about why they're chasing their tails to pay for a big house they can't really enjoy because they're working so damn hard to pay for it."

"Like us, you mean," I said. "We were so certain we needed that big house, but it was killing us to pay for it. And now we're just as happy sitting in Mrs. Mattingley's house, renting! Aren't we, Pieter?" I said, tongue in cheek, shooting Pieter a look as I spoke. The three of us stopped. Hazen took a seat on a park bench, taking in the postcard view of sailors and rowers enjoying the late morning.

"Exactly. When I look at the statistics, I wonder whether we haven't arrived at a natural point of resistance. Back in the early 1970s, Americans were paying 15 to 20 percent of their incomes for housing. But by the 1990s, we were devoting nearly 30 percent of our incomes to the roof over our heads. We might have reached a point where we simply don't want to pay any more for housing."

"So you're saying that housing has become a bad investment," Pieter said.

"It's neither a good nor a bad investment," Hazen replied crisply. "I'd suggest that it's not an investment at all. It's a place to live, period. You boomers cannot count on your home to be a retirement nest egg like your parents' generation did. Now, you could liken buying a house to taking a very expensive cruise. You're buying yourself a pricey life experience, but you're probably not going to make any money out of the deal. In fact, given the amount of money you shell out in maintaining your house—painting, reroofing, replacing furnaces and plumbing—it may very well be costing you money. If you plan on living in one spot your entire adult life, it might be worth your while to buy. But if you're going to move around during your stay on the planet, it may make sense to avoid buying and rent instead. That's what I was talking about the first time I met you, Meredith. You two are smart to rent until you decide what your next step will be. The trick is understanding your needs—and not being driven by your wants."

"I don't know, Hazen," Pieter said. "I would feel a lot better owning my own home." I got a look back as he spoke. After nearly fifteen years of marriage, we both had "the look" down pat.

Hazen said, "That's certainly the way we have been brought up, and the vast majority of us who now rent hope to be able to purchase a home someday. But home ownership may not be the way to go in the future. And you shouldn't be considering your house as a pension plan. What worked for your parents is not necessarily going to work for you. Times change." He pushed himself up from the bench and started to walk. "Come along. I want to show you my crow's nest."

"Crow's nest?" I asked.

"You know, a lookout point. I have a favorite spot that I visit to watch the passing of the seasons over Massachusetts," Hazen explained as we turned off the boardwalk, crossing busy Storrow Drive by bridge and joining the tourists admiring the architecture in the Back Bay.

"Hazen, how do you explain the hot spots in the current real estate market? San Francisco, for example," Pieter asked.

"Good point. Do you remember I said earlier that the housing market is becoming more like a stock market? Well, housing prices in San Francisco are a perfect example of that. There's currently about a $100,000 gap between comparable housing in Boston and San Francisco. Demographics drives the San Francisco market ever faster. But it's not baby boom demographics. California is experiencing a boom because of migration, both from within the states and without. It's a choice spot for people who appreciate San Francisco's history and character, combined with its attractiveness to business. It has a strong financial base, and Silicon Valley is only an hour away. Add to that the climate, the universities, and its international flair, and you have a very attractive place to live. San Francisco is one of the niche markets I've been telling you about. But you can look a lot closer for a niche market. Think about your old neighborhood, Concord."

"That's a joke, comparing Concord to San Francisco," Pieter retorted.

"Agreed. There are vast differences in the prices. But I'm talking about comparing Concord to other suburbs surrounding Boston. Certainly, there is some hi-tech industry in Concord, which makes it a niche market on its own, although towns like Southboro would probably fall into this category more aptly. What makes Concord attractive to people is its proximity to Boston, its school system, its history and character, and the fact that it has always signified the quintessential 'successful' town. There are plenty of other niche markets out there, though. I'm going to show you one now," Hazen said. We found ourselves standing in front of the Hancock Tower, a sixty-floor angular glass structure in the downtown core.

Pieter laughed. "You're not going to tell us to buy an office tower, are you?"

"No. My crow's nest is in here," he said. "Whenever I come here, I think of the tourist trolley buses that drive past every ten minutes or so. The tour guides love to quote stats about the tower, like the fact that the original glass all had to be replaced because it kept breaking. Now, over 10,000 panes of safety glass frame the building; the grey tinting is what allows it to take on the reflection of the surrounding buildings. Did you know there are thirty double-deck elevators inside and that 7,500 passengers can be transported in only fifteen minutes?"

"What would we do without your numbers, Hazen?" I asked, with a nudge, as we headed into the elevator with a group of tourists.

He laughed. "Well, statistics aside, there's no arguing the view on a clear day. This is where I come to admire the land and the sea." After a few high-speed seconds, we exited the elevator high above the city.

"Hazen, if you look straight there," said Pieter, pointing into the distance, "that's the way to our cottage."

"Odd you should mention that, Pieter. I think second homes, like cottages, will develop as a healthy niche market."

"Yes, I remember you mentioned that in your seminar the other night," I said.

"It's another boomer thing," Hazen continued. "Traditionally, the over-forty-five crowd is the biggest group of second-home owners. That's where the boomers are headed. Of course, country homes will never hit the heights that city homes did. There are just not enough well-off boomers to fund that kind of white-hot market. But I'd keep a close eye on country properties that are close to big cities or situated on a particularly appealing site. For example, consider smaller towns around Boston, and look at hot leisure spots like Vermont, Cape Ann, and Cape Cod."

"We're glad we've kept our cottage," I said. "It's a great place for us to go with the kids. The older they get, the better it is to keep them active—swimming, hiking, cross-country skiing—whatever the season. Plus, it's a nice spot for us to entertain friends. Speaking of which, would you consider coming up for a weekend this summer?"

"Meredith, I'd be delighted. I've always considered New Hampshire to be a lovely place to relax," Hazen answered. "Before we leave my lookout, I want to talk a little bit about commercial real estate, and I want you to tell me what you don't see."

"What do you mean?" Pieter asked.

"There's something that's very nearly missing from the Boston skyline. In fact, they've more or less disappeared from the skylines of many U.S. cities in the past few years," said Hazen.

"I love riddles, but I can't figure out this one," I said.

"Construction cranes," Hazen said. "Courtesy of the boomers, back in the 1970s there were cranes everywhere on the Boston skyline. That was no surprise. At that time, boomers were flocking into the workplace in droves and developers were hustling to build places for them to work. The early-1990s brought some tough times for landlords. Currently, the market's picked up and those landlords are heaving a sigh of relief as their office towers fill back up. But, the boom is not back with the same intensity. Many experts are questioning how strong the demand is and how long it will last. As you know, technology has allowed many workers who used to inhabit these office towers to work at home now."

"I'm a perfect example of that phenomenon," I said. "My basement is my office."

"I predict we'll see a lot more of that. In a similar vein, a lot of companies are deciding that they don't have to be downtown to conduct their business. That brings me back to Concord and Southboro. Hi-tech companies don't need to be within spitting distance of the Hancock Tower. Space is cheaper in the suburbs and workers like to be able to live close to their workplace."

"That's another example of a niche market," agreed Pieter.

"Exactly," replied Hazen. "And now, I'm getting hungry, and I could use a café au lait. What about you?"

"Sounds great," I answered, following Hazen back down to Copley Square, anticipating the hit of caffeine.

We continued our discussion at a small café on Newbury Street.

"The key is to look forward and not allow the recent past to cloud our vision about the real estate market and its potential," said Hazen, biting into his scrambled eggs.

"I'm intrigued by your idea of real estate turning into a sort of stock market," Pieter remarked.

"Take a look as we walk back to the 'T,'" said Hazen. "There's a great niche market—courtesy of the aging boomers—sitting right here in the form of upscale condominiums."

"But I thought condo prices were in the doldrums," I said.

"Actually, the condo market has rebounded to a very healthy state following the lows it sunk to in the late-1980s and 1990s. The market was hit very hard by the bust because it had been so overvalued and so over-built in the previous boom cycle," said Hazen. "But there is an upsurge in upscale condos. I have a friend who is a real-tor, and he tells me that he has heard several stories of empty nesters returning to Boston for high-style living with all the amenities after the kids have grown and gone. Now that type of real estate—the kind with a great view and lo-cation—is limited in supply. In fact, I bought one two years ago. I currently rent it out. I'd be living there now if it wasn't for my garden."

"What about that Will Rogers chestnut about buying land because they aren't making any more of it?" I asked.

"Old Will was right about certain markets at certain times. Cottages and condos can be an example of that. But generally, his comment is way off base. The size of the boom made it appear as though real estate was scarce in this country. In reality, supply was just trying to catch up to the demands of the boomers. And supply does catch up to demand eventually. Then prices cor-rect. That's what you've always got to keep in mind."

Our chat continued, the waiter kept bringing coffee, and the morning gave way to the afternoon. Not a bad way to learn about our finances.

11

Interested in Interest Rates?

I had a bee in my bonnet. Our discussions with Hazen had raised serious concerns in my mind about whether Pieter and I were doing enough to provide for the kids' education. Hazen had questioned our current arrangement of placing the children's funds in T-bonds, and my recent conversation with my friend Heather had added to my concerns. Pieter and I were absolutely committed to giving Malcolm and Emily the opportunity of attending college. Of course we'd expect them to find summer jobs in order to throw some money in the education pot, but the final responsibility rested with the two of us. We needed to be doing things differently.

I was turning the issue over in my mind as I walked down to Hank's. I was planning on tackling the bubblegum-pink bathroom, and I needed a paintbrush. It felt good to be outside. Summer was in the air at last. I exchanged smiles with the people I passed on the sidewalk. That pinched look of winter had faded into history.

As I neared Hank's, I saw Hazen and Hank standing outside the store, heads bent together in intense conversation. Fertilizer. They were engrossed in debating the merits of fertilizer, I realized as I got within earshot. How could two men get so worked up about fertilizer? Must be a guy thing.

"Hello, gentlemen. It sure looks as though the nice weather is here to stay," I said, strolling up to them.

Neither man seemed to mind the interruption. Hank asked if I could use some help, and I explained my need for a paintbrush. He hustled inside to find me one.

"I wanted to thank you for the real estate tour on the weekend," I said to Hazen. "I think we've started to find some answers to the many questions we have about our financial future, but it sure is confusing."

"It's a riddle wrapped in a mystery inside an enigma, as Winston Churchill would have said," replied Hazen. "People don't get good answers because they don't stop and think of the good questions they need to ask. You and Pieter are at the beginning of the process—starting to identify the questions."

That was the best opening I'd heard in a long time. So I jumped in with my next good question. "Hazen, Pieter and I are having nagging doubts about investing for the kids' education. We really don't know if we've invested properly and how much we should be aiming to save. As you know, so far everything is in T-bonds."

"'Saving is a wonderful thing, especially if your parents do it for you.' Churchill said that too. But seriously,

Meredith, your concerns about saving for your children's education is a perfect lead into the next major topic that I want to discuss with you and Pieter: interest rates."

"How will a lecture on interest rates help us figure out the educational investment conundrum?" I asked.

"Interest rate levels affect just about every major decision you'll make in life," Hazen explained. "I started out with the real estate tour because that's a commodity everybody can see, feel, and understand; and it's also something that your generation has already affected. But interest rates are a little more difficult to understand. You can't see interest rates but, believe me, they matter in your life. And boomers have had a major influence on interest rates for the past twenty years. That influence will continue until the day they die."

"So how should we tackle this topic?"

"What's on the DeMarco agenda tonight after the kids have gone to bed?"

I chuckled. "Economics 101, I guess."

"Economics 101 with the Armstrong twist—what they didn't teach you at college. I'll be over at nine o'clock. No spirits tonight. This will be a very serious chat. Like I said, the price of money is one commodity that affects just about every decision we make." With that, Hazen was off down the street. I went into Hank's to pick up my brush, steeling myself to head home and tackle the pink bathroom.

———

At 9:00 Emily was tucked into bed and Malcolm was upstairs reading a novel for a book report. True to his word, Hazen knocked at the door at the stroke of nine. He had a file folder tucked under his arm.

"What's in your folder?" I asked.

"Just a couple of charts to illustrate some points," he answered.

"That doesn't sound nearly as exciting as your silver dollar routine," I replied.

He laughed. "Maybe not—but they'll have a bigger impact on your financial well-being."

Pieter emerged from the computer room in the basement.

"Okay, you two, let's get down to business," said Hazen. "We've got a lot of ground to cover this evening. Like I told Meredith this morning, interest rates aren't as easy to understand as real estate. Most economists never figure out where they're headed next. That's why I've brought a couple of charts from my presentation to show you how your generation has affected interest rates."

"Can I get you something, Hazen? Some tea maybe?" Pieter asked.

"No thanks, Pete, I want to get right to this. Okay, interest rates have a profound influence in our day-to-day lives. Think about it. Mortgage rates, savings rates, how you invest. Can you afford to buy a house? Where should you be investing your children's money? Where should you be investing your own dollars? All these decisions are predicated on interest rate levels. Interest rates are, after all, nothing more than the price of borrowing money. Interest rates go up and money costs more to borrow. When this happens, a lot of the things we do become more expensive—like buying a house.

If there's one commodity that boomers have hit hard, it's money. It's the same old story. All of you boomers showed up needing to borrow money to finance your first steps into adulthood."

I glanced over at Pieter, who was sporting a big smile. "It didn't take long to cut to the chase and bring those boomers into the discussion," he said.

"I couldn't let you down," Hazen retorted. "Now let's start from the beginning." With that, Hazen pulled out his first chart, handing copies to Pieter and me. "This is a simple graph showing the ratio of spenders to savers over the past forty years. As a rule of thumb, older people tend to lend to younger people. Spenders are defined as 25- to 34-year-olds. They're the folks who are borrowing money to buy homes and start up their households and families. Savers are older, aged 45 to 54. They've established the households and have moved into their peak earning years. We're in equilibrium when we have the same number of spenders as savers. For years and years, interest rates were not only stable but also very low. Back in the 1950s and 1960s, we were in equilibrium—equal number of savers and spenders."

"That seems simple enough to follow," I said. "But what happened here?" I pointed to a huge upward leap in the ratio during the mid-1980s.

"That surge means we had many more spenders than savers in the country during that time period," Hazen explained. "Let's look back a bit. In the '60s, rates continued to be very stable, but then the early-'70s rolled around. We had always had the reputation for being a stable place. The 1970s changed all that and the world was left scratching its head. What happened? Simple—the boom hit. The peace and love years were over and it was time to go to work. Boomers were young adults entering the economy and starting their lives. They needed to borrow money to buy cars, clothes, stereos, houses, all the things you need when you set up your own household."

"Aha—back to the boom," remarked Pieter.

"It would have been great if this enormous generation came into the economy as well-heeled fifty-year-olds. But, of course, we all enter the market as twenty-year-olds in the same basic state: broke. And the young boomers put incredible pressure on money. Now, if you look at what happens on the graph, you see that explains the surge in the number of spenders that you pointed out, Meredith. Spenders ruled the marketplace, overwhelming the number of savers. The equation is simple: more spenders than savers, big demand for money, lots of borrowing. Put it all together and you get higher interest rates. It's all a question of supply and demand. Remember, money is a commodity like any other. The number of spenders kept exploding and peaked in the mid- to late-1980s. Think about it. This makes very good sense. The birth rate peaked in the mid-1950s. The birth rate tells us the total number of births divided by the size of the population. A high birth rate in the 1950s means that those children were entering the economy in the early-1980s as spenders—lots and lots of spenders. Very predictable. After the peak in the 1980s, you see that the ratio of spenders versus savers begins to drop.

Once again, very predictable. The boom is aging and moving into their savings years."

"This is exactly what Ruth was telling me the other day, that boomers are just beginning to move into savings mode," I said.

"Exactly," Hazen replied. "Now we're in the late-1990s, boomers are aging, and it's no great surprise that interest rates are low, reaching the levels we experienced in the 1960s. We're moving back to equilibrium, where we have an equal number of spenders and savers. But there's more. And this is the great news. We are poised to enter another period of disequilibrium. We're going to get out of whack again, but this time savers are going to outnumber spenders. And guess what's going to happen?"

"That's easy. The demand for money is going to lessen and that's going to affect interest rates, keeping them nice and low," I answered.

"Good—you're getting it." Hazen smiled. "In the early-'80s, our economy was in a nasty recession and, if you recall, we came flying out of it. Boomers were just entering the economy and they were spending like crazy. Along with the government, they deserve a lot of the credit for buying us out of that recession." Hazen paused, waiting for us to catch his pun.

"In the early-'90s," he continued, "we had an equally nasty recession, but this time around the boomers had started to shift to savings mode. Not so funny this time. There wasn't a horde of young boomers waiting in the wings to come into the economy and spend, spend, spend. And because incomes were declining or stagnating during this period, they didn't have a lot of extra money to spend. Many analysts suggested something had gone awry in our economy. I think they should consider the fact that your generation got ten years older. For many, saving is just beginning to become a priority. So here's my first great prediction of the night. And you can take this one to the bank."

"Come on, come on. Spit it out," heckled Pieter.

"By and large, interest rates will likely stay low for the rest of your adult lives," Hazen concluded.

"How can you be so certain of that?" Pieter asked. "It would be great news for businesses like my own. Anybody who borrows is going to love this."

"My certainty comes from the next graph I want to show you," said Hazen, handing each of us another page. "You might remember this one from my seminar. It shows you the birth rate and the inflation rate over the past few decades. It's no surprise that about twenty years after the spike in the birth rate—that's you boomers—the inflation rate spiked. It's a perfect mirror image."

"At your seminar, I must admit you lost me with this graph," Pieter said. "What's the relationship between inflation and interest rates?"

"Inflation is a continuing rise in the prices of what we buy and consume. It reduces the purchasing power of our money. Interest rates measure the demand for money. Generally, they move in sync: high inflation rates, high interest rates. Let's have a look at this graph. The assumption is that we're born and it takes twenty years for us to grow up and join the economy. As we take our place as adults, we borrow money and buy a lot of stuff. When the boomers hit the economy, they threw it into a tizzy, causing disequilibrium. For a time, there were far more spenders than savers. That meant money was in short supply, bidding up the price—interest rates. And money in motion causes inflation. Boomers were putting pressure on goods—bidding up the prices. Add to this an increase in the volume of money and credit, and you get inflation—price levels rise. My conclusion? If you have a dramatic, protracted spike in the birth rate, you'll have rising inflation about twenty years later. You with me?"

"So far," Pieter said and I nodded.

"Well, that explains the perfect correlation—the birth rate in this country is tracked almost precisely by inflation with a lag of twenty-four years. That's no coincidence. That allows me to make my bold statement about continued low interest rates. Why? Take a look at the birth rate in the last thirty years," he said, pointing to his graph.

"It's very clear," Pieter answered. "It's stuck at a very low rate."

"Right. The trend of our birth rate has been in decline for the last three decades. There was a slight increase in the late-1980s and early-1990s as many boomers had their children. This blip has now tailed off as this generation approaches middle age. There is no new surge in our birth rate that will contribute to inflation in the future. Now I know that economists will throw models and analyses at this, but in the end, it all boils down to people. Interest rates are affected by people. Because of the current demographics in this country, we will have low interest rates for years."

"I know you talked about this at the seminar the other night, but how do you square away your theory with the fact that we're always hearing in the media—that savings rates are in free-fall in this country?" I inquired.

"Right. When economists talk about the savings rate, they're referring to the amount that people put away as a percentage of after-tax income. Many experts now agree that this is far too narrow a measure of savings. Looking at the big picture—at all of our assets, not just what we save out of our incomes—gives us a clearer understanding of how we're preparing for our financial futures. And between 1992 and 1995, median net worth rose 6.8 percent. Interestingly—but not surprisingly when one understands demographics—the share of financial assets in families' total asset holdings has steadily risen, while the share of family assets held in nonfinancial forms, including investment real estate and vehicles, has declined. Let's face it—financial decisions of boomers are influenced by two key things: the cost of a college education for their children and the realization that they must begin to save for retirement."

"Yes, that all makes good sense to me, but I've always heard that our interest rates are dependent on what's happening around the world. It's a global economy, isn't it?"

"Good point. Of course, U.S. interest rates are tied into the world economy, but those ties will loosen somewhat as we age. We have always been a young country relative to others in the world. It costs governments a pretty penny to educate and groom a young population to take its place in the economy. Our government ran up a large public debt to tend to its needs. But I'd suggest that these trends will reverse—and our prolonged, relatively low birth rate is one culprit. Make no mistake, there have been others too. Look at the huge run-up in defense spending back in the Vietnam and Cold War decades, for example. Now, this country, as it ages, is on its way to balancing its budget. And the government better get on with reducing the budget deficit pretty quickly or risk irritating voters. A recent Gallup poll shows that reducing the federal deficit is a top priority for American investors. Remember, it all boils down to your people profile. Old people lend to young people, and similarly, old countries lend to young ones. We just have to look at the long term."

"So how can we use this information?" I asked.

"Having that long-term view gives us the ability to invest wisely and profitably. Let's take the kids' education fund that you mentioned to me this morning, Meredith. At this stage, with the kids so far away from actually going to college, you should be avoiding those T-bonds like the plague. The rates they pay are going to stay low, but the cost of an education is set to skyrocket."

"Where should we be putting our money?" I asked.

"That's where you need an adviser," Hazen said. "But I'll give you a hint. A financial adviser should be recommending setting up trust accounts for the children and purchasing good mutual funds to put into those accounts. Something conservative that can grow at a level sufficient to supply a nice pot of capital for the children's schooling. I'd suggest an equity fund—that's a fund composed of stocks. It has the potential for providing more growth than, say, a bond fund, and its tax treatment makes a lot of financial sense. In simple terms, you and Pieter may not be liable for taxes payable down the road. Your adviser will probably also tell you about the new educational funding vehicle called the Education IRA. This IRA is for the purpose of paying the higher education expenses of a designated beneficiary—in your case, your children. But you should discuss all this with your financial adviser."

"What are some of the other investments we should consider?" Pieter asked. "Why would you recommend an equity fund as opposed to a bond fund?"

"The available mutual funds are as varied as the type of financial instruments on the market. But let's not put the cart before the horse. I'd like to spend an entire evening canvassing the issue of mutual funds. But all this talk about interest rates leads me directly to the subject of bonds. Interest rates and bonds are inextricably linked, you know," Hazen said.

"I sort of knew that, but I'm not quite sure on the details," I said. "How does it work?"

"Let's start by figuring out what a bond is. Companies raise money in two ways. They sell ownership in the company: stocks. Or they borrow money: bonds. A bond represents a debt that the company promises to repay to the holder of the bond. It's a promise to pay the holder a specified amount of interest for a specified time and to repay the loan when it becomes due. Government savings bonds are odd ducks—they can be redeemed almost any time but can't be sold to other investors. On the other hand, most bonds can't be redeemed before maturity but they can be sold to other investors through a securities dealer, like an investment broker. Legally, a bond is less risky than a stock. A corporation is bound to pay its bondholders before it pays its shareholders. But bonds still have their risks—not all corporations will be able to repay their debts. However, as we've discussed previously, there are plenty of other risks besides legal ones. I'd argue that it's financially riskier to invest in bonds because there's not going to be the same opportunity for the big returns that stocks will yield in the future," Hazen explained. "But you must have an idea of what you will need for a nest egg in the future, and there will probably be some bonds in that basket. It all depends on the asset mix you need, the return you will need to make on your investments, the income you need your investments to generate—and when you'll be needing that income. This is also something a financial adviser can help you with."

"I can see bonds are tied to interest rates, but how do fluctuations in rates affect the price of bonds?" asked Pieter.

"It's actually fairly straightforward," Hazen responded. "Bonds work inversely to interest rates. Rates up, bond prices down, and vice versa. The key element is to understand why it works that way. Let's keep it simple. Let's say you had a bond that promised to pay 10 percent to its holder. Now remember, bonds are not like CDs. Bonds are very liquid. By that I mean you can buy and sell them very easily. Let's say you buy a municipal bond at 10 percent, then rates go up to 12 percent. You can sell that bond, but keep in mind that a buyer can now get 12 percent in the market. The result? The value of your bond has dropped because you have a bond that will earn you only 10 percent when the market pays 12 percent. When you sell your bond, you'll have to discount the price to attract a buyer. The opposite occurs if rates fall. You're going to do very well with your 10 percent bond if rates go down to 7 percent."

"When interest rates are low, like they are now, should we invest in bonds?" I asked.

"Actually, bonds are currently a very attractive long-term investment and should probably be included as a portion of your investment portfolio," Hazen replied. "Here's the reason: although rates appear to be low, they'll likely go even lower. That's because of where the boomers are today. Boomers are just on the verge of their big savings push—those are the savings that I predict will contribute to keeping interest rates low in this country. Real interest rates—subtract the inflation rate from the interest rate and that gives you the 'real' interest rate—are still historically high. Real rates have lots of room to decline, and since bonds move in the opposite direction to the interest rate, that means that bonds have lots of room to increase in price, making them a good part of a portfolio designed for the long term."

"Why the long term?" I asked.

"Whatever you decide, wherever you put your money, the key element of your investing plan must be the long-term view. The long-term perspective will keep you from making major mistakes. And you cannot think long term in this country without considering the impact of the baby boom," Hazen stated. "Here, I have an interesting story about bonds to support the long-term view. A few years ago, many Americans found that their once-cherished CD had fallen on hard times. The double-digit interest rates of the 1980s were long gone. This left many in a quandary—they had no clue where to put their money. They didn't have the long-term view, so they couldn't anticipate that just as the boomers once brought high rates, now they were responsible for lower ones. They had no plan, so they just rolled their money. Many of these 'CD refugees' turned to bonds as an alternative. Just about every bond had a sensational return because interest rates had fallen. But in 1994, after rates had fallen for about a decade, they spiked up a bit. That scared these new bondholders. Shaken up, many of them dumped their newly purchased bonds."

"That was because they didn't have a long-term plan," Pieter stated.

"Precisely. Remember what the boom is telling us. Low interest rates will be here to stay for a long time. But that doesn't mean that there won't be the odd upward spike in the interest rate along the way. Like you were saying earlier, Pete, it's a global economy. A drastic piece of international news could cause a leap in interest rates. Similarly, look what the Gulf War crisis did to the financial markets in this country. That could easily happen again. But keep in mind that news is news—it's the newest thing that happens and, generally speaking, it's eclipsed by the next newest thing to come along. Though news can affect interest rates in the short term, we want to look at the long-term trend—things that are going to stay around for a long time. The baby boom is one of those things that has enormous staying power. You have to learn to ride out the short-term blips. And having a well-thought-out long-term view of the world gives you the knowledge and instincts to stick with your investments."

"And you have to know what the boomers are doing," I joked.

"Watch them like a hawk—that's my advice," Hazen retorted. "You're getting it. You and the rest of your generation are poised to set off a savings campaign the likes of which this country has never seen."

"So why do we keep reading all these stories about the boomers' big debts?" asked Pieter.

"Well, there's no doubt that the past few years have been tough on individuals' incomes, and levels of family debt have risen. But to my mind, the media can't see the forest for the trees." Hazen chuckled. "Like many unsuccessful investors, the media are notoriously shortsighted. They look at the here and now. Well, the majority of boomers have not yet hit their peak savings years. So, for the media, savings isn't a story—yet. Your generation has just begun to move into its savings years and debt levels are high, both in the private and public sectors. Like many American households, the governments of this country are all struggling to get their debts and deficits under control. But that's exactly what you'd expect. Getting the boomers educated and launched into the economy was an extremely expensive venture for the government. But now we get to reap the benefits." Hazen rubbed his hands together.

"How's that?" I asked.

"Today, this country has a well-educated, middle-aged work force. Our productivity is set to explode. But let's look at those debt levels. Like I said before, older people lend to younger people, and similarly, older countries lend to younger countries. Well, after the Second World War, we were a very young country—courtesy of the baby boom. Between 1950 and 1970, the median age—that's the point at which half the population is below that age and half above—dropped to under thirty years. Since 1970, the median age has been on a steep upward climb. In 1994, the median age was over thirty-four. By 2030, experts suggest that, under the right conditions, the median age could hit nearly forty."

"That's the boom driving all those statistics," I commented.

"You got it," Hazen said. "We added almost 77 million babies to this country pretty quickly. Now, because of our lowered birth rate, America is aging at an incredible clip. Many analysts will call me a heretic, but I believe that the government will tame its reliance on borrowed money and pay down its debt. As they age, this crazed group of spenders from the 1970s and 1980s will put just as much pressure on savings as they once did on spending. Retirement accounts will soak up much of the savings of the huge boomer generation. And lots of that money will go into bonds and stocks. The savings years are just upon us.

"Here's something for you to try with your friends. Ask them what their major financial concerns are these days. I'll bet they list them this way. One, paying off their mortgage and other debts. Two, saving for retirement. Three, putting away some cash for their children's education. Saving, saving, saving. The media are going to have a field day with this in ten years' time. They'll be writing about the great economic miracle in America. Keep in mind nothing ever really changed; the boom grew up."

"I'd support your prediction about what our friends are thinking about financially," I said. "When I phoned around for some financial ideas, they were all talking about saving."

"It's time. Take a look at what they're doing and invest accordingly. On the interest rate side, that might mean buying a bond for as long a term as possible. Rates could fall further yet. Our future is the mirror image of our recent past."

"But, Hazen, if all these savers can't get a decent return on bonds, surely they'll be looking elsewhere to invest their money," said Pieter.

"They're already doing it. Boomers are starting to pressure the stock market. It's the next thing and, not coincidentally, it's the next thing I want to discuss with you," Hazen replied, glancing down at his watch. "Yikes, it's almost eleven o'clock. I want to get home and watch the news. Why don't you two mull this over and then, while it's still fresh in your minds, we'll get together at my place to discuss the next commodity: the stock market."

With that, he collected his charts and bade us goodnight. We watched him amble across the street before we began to turn off the lights.

"Meredith, I've got a couple of things I want to talk to you about," said Pieter as we climbed the stairs. "Today I phoned the accountant we use at work and made an appointment to discuss our tax arrangements."

"Thanks, Pieter. That's been on my mind since I spoke to Heather. I want to see if I can write off some of our housing expenses. What else is on your list?" I asked, sitting down on the edge of the bed and slipping off my shoes.

"I've been mulling over all this boomer stuff, and there's one issue that I keep returning to," he said.

"What's that?"

"When I was at the library the other day, I picked up a couple of books by Faith Popcorn: *The Popcorn Report* and *Clicking*. They talk about what's affecting our lives—interesting things."

"Yes, I've heard of those books. Faith Popcorn is the one who talks about cocooning. That idea's a little stale, isn't it? We've been cocooning for over a decade, since Malcolm was born. I'm waiting for the butterflies to emerge. I'm sure Hazen could tell us who'll benefit from that transformation."

"Cocooning isn't what intrigues me. Evidently, she's set up a brain trust of experts who act as her advisers on major challenges facing society. She pulls in the appropriate experts depending on the issue she's considering and the solutions she needs to provide to her clients."

"Sounds like a good idea, but isn't it just a form of brainstorming?" I asked.

"Right. It's a really simple approach, and that's exactly why it hit me. Why should only people like Faith Popcorn have access to a brain trust? Why couldn't I design a product that would give boomers on-line access to a network of experts to answer whatever questions were on their minds? Not only would it be a time saver—and we all know boomers are notoriously short of that commodity—but it would give boomers truly up-to-date access to information, better and easier than looking things up in a book. It could be used for a wide variety of reasons—business, personal, academic, you name it," Pieter said, pulling his sweater over his head.

"Sounds good to me. You know, sometimes the simple approach is the one that's overlooked," I said.

"And you know, I even have a name for it: Boomer-Bytes."

"Boy, you're taking this boomer stuff seriously." I rolled into bed. "But that's enough for tonight. Time for bed. As you know, we boomers are aging and need our sleep."

12

Taking Stock of the Stock Market

As late spring blossomed, our lives moved into summertime mode. Pieter was occupied with BoomerBytes and his positive outlook was back, along with a renewed interest in his work. There had been no great breakthroughs, yet things were back in perspective. The kids jumped into summer sports— baseball, soccer, biking, skateboarding, and rollerblading. Our evenings were filled with practices, and a jumble of bats, balls, and stinky sneakers crammed the front hall. Ruth and I had launched our focus groups, and I was working four or five full days each week. We were busy, but it was a good busy. The four of us were doing the things we wanted to, back in charge of our lives.

Despite our level of activity, Hazen had inspired us to keep up on our financial homework. Slowly but surely, we were plodding through our reading list and making the rounds of financial advisers, interviewing each of them. We still hadn't made any decisions, however. We wanted to hear Hazen's final lectures before we embarked on our financial journey. He'd promised us a couple more sessions covering the stock market and mutual funds. But we were on hold for the week. Hazen was away, tending to clients in Cincinnati. We'd been given the task of looking after the British Gentlemen's Club, as we referred to his house. Ever the snoop, I checked out the place as I watered his plants. I was intrigued by a charming photo of Ruth, Dylan, and Hazen, taken on the occasion of Dylan's graduation—from high school, I guessed. It was nice to know that their friendship included Dylan. That's something I particularly liked about Hazen. He always had the time for Malcolm and Emily. I'd often see Malcolm skateboarding after school,up and down the sidewalk in front of Hazen's house, the two of them chatting as Hazen gardened. He would have made a good father, I thought.

Upon returning from his trip, Hazen invited us over for dinner. The evening was designated Stock Market Night. This subject, he told us, was the one that excited him most these days because, in his opinion, the boomers were poised to hit the stock market—hard!

Hazen had a broad smile on his face as he opened the door to Pieter and me. "How are my two favorite pupils?" he asked. "Thanks for looking after the plants. They're healthier than when I'm home."

"That's the thing about houseplants, Hazen. Just like people, they need a little bit of positive attention," I replied.

Hazen showed us into the living room, where appetizers were laid out, along with an open bottle of red wine. "Nothing like a fine wine to stimulate the mind," he quipped.

"Thomas Jefferson, right?" said Pieter.

Hazen laughed. "No, I think it was Julio Gallo." Hazen hadn't lost a step on his swing through Ohio. "Well, he who hesitates is lost, so let's get onto the topic for the evening. Boomers are headed for the stock market, and that's where we should be going as well. I'm going to break this evening's discussion into two segments because the boomers affect the market in two distinct ways: directly and indirectly. You're now set to hit it indirectly as you begin to pour your savings into stocks. But you've been hitting it directly from the moment you were born. Your huge generation has had an enormous impact on the corporations that list their stocks on the market, and that influence is going to continue until the day you die. Tonight, I'm going to lead off with the indirect effect you're about to land on the market."

"I don't know, Hazen," I mused. "I'm still quite scared of the market. My parents were Depression children. You didn't play the market. You know, a penny at hand is worth a dollar at a distance."

"You're not wrong, Meredith. You're right to be cautious of the market. But I never 'play' the market. I make intelligent investments there. The market is like any potential investment field—there are good places to invest and there are lousy places. But you don't stay off the field because it has some soft spots. You just stay clear of those soft spots. Over time, the market has been an excellent long-term performer—the best, in fact. While the statistics show that increasing numbers of Americans are entering the stock market either directly by purchasing publicly traded stocks or indirectly through mutual funds and retirement accounts, there are still many who avoid it like the plague. I'd suggest that quite a few of them think like you do. They avoid the market because of the volatility. But that's a short-term view. Yes, there are corrections. That's what the market calls declines of 10 percent or more. And there have been plenty of them, about one every two years. The trick is learning to live through them, hold on to your stocks, and wait for the market to rebound. Think about the long haul and stay the course.

"I think when you hear what I have to say, you will understand why we need to be in the stock market to prepare ourselves for a healthy financial future. Your parents were lucky. Remember the effect of the boom on real estate and interest rates."

"Too bad we don't have that kind of luck—a tiny generation follows us," said Pieter.

"Hold it right there," Hazen said. "You've reaped enormous benefits simply by being part of this mammoth generation. Let me tell you, if you had a child ready to enter the work force for the first time, you'd think the boomers had been extraordinarily lucky, sitting there with all the jobs, making it really tough for this younger, smaller generation to get a toehold in the job market."

"You're right," I said. "I'm glad Malcolm and Emily are the ages they are. Maybe a few of the boomers will be out of the way by the time they get ready to look for full-time work."

"Funny, this dark view of the world that you boomers seem to share and that the media love to promote," Hazen mused. "Do you know that just before the Second World War was the last time North Americans held this same attitude, that the world couldn't deliver for their children, that things were getting worse? That generation had lived through the Depression. They saw themselves at the brink of war, big changes were on the horizon. Some American commentators have pointed out that our society is at the brink of equally profound changes—those wrought by technology. It's all about change. When we as a society face mammoth change, we get scared. Keep in mind that the last generation to have these dreary thoughts about their children's future were your grandparents, parents of one of the luckiest generations ever to arrive on the face of this planet. But enough about the job market. Let's talk stocks," said Hazen, reaching for his glass. "First, do you know what stocks are?"

"Well, we've been reading up on this stuff, you know, but tell us anyhow," Pieter replied.

"A stock is a certificate representing ownership in a company. Common stock does carry voting privileges. You can go to the company's annual meeting and have your say. Ownership carries with it certain risks. Principally, you're not guaranteed a specific return as is the case with bonds or other fixed-interest securities. If the company declares bankruptcy, you'll probably be kissing your investment goodbye. Am I alleviating your nervousness, Meredith?" Hazen asked, smiling.

"Not a whole lot, Hazen," I retorted.

"Relax, it gets better as we go along. Now, where was I? Oh yes . . . There are different types of stock, representing different kinds of companies: income and growth stocks. Typically, you can count on income stocks, issued by established companies, to provide a fairly generous dividend—money that is distributed out of a company's profits to its shareholders. Then there's growth stock— stock of a company that's got great potential for growth and expansion. Your profit may not come in dividends. In this case, you're counting on the price of the stock itself to rise."

"Are growth stocks riskier than income stocks?" I asked.

"Sure. Growth stocks are issued by companies in their initial stages of development. As with any new business, there are no guarantees and, as a result, the stock prices may fluctuate a great deal. Purchasers of growth stocks, however, are counting on the greater up- side potential of those stocks. Income stocks—issued by banks and utilities, for example—are generally very sta- ble in price and pay higher dividends on a regular basis. Income stocks are issued by companies that have been around for years. They're often referred to as blue chip stocks." He paused. "I should also mention preferred stocks," he continued. "They are a class of shares that entitle the owners to a specified dollar amount in the case of the liquidation of the company that has issued them. A company raises debt capital with them, but they are accounted for as equities. They act more like bonds than stocks. Given that characteristic, I think preferred shares won't hold any great appeal for boomer investors for the next twenty-odd years." He took a sip of wine.

"Let me explain that last comment," Hazen continued. "Another thing I want you to understand, before we get to the influence that boomers are going to have on the market, is the relationship between interest rates, the bond market, and the stock market. Like I told you the other day, they're all inextricably linked. The bond market is the horse; the stock market is the cart. When bond prices go down, that means higher yields because interest rates have gone up. Investment dollars are then drawn away from the stock market because attractive returns can be made safely outside the market. But remember what I told you about interest rates?"

"You said they were going to stay low for the next couple of decades because of the saving force the boomers would be bringing to the economy," I answered.

"Exactly. And in the long term, that makes bonds look fairly unattractive. Once interest rates go low and stay low, bond prices stagnate—they do nothing."

"So if there's a prolonged period of low interest rates," Pieter said, "that will take money away from the bond market?"

"That's the conventional wisdom. But don't forget, a huge amount of savings is going to hit both markets. You invest in bonds and stocks for different reasons and at different stages in your life," Hazen explained. "I would never advocate a portfolio without a mixture of both stocks and bonds. The balance you strike will depend on your needs and wants at the time. Let me give you an example. As you near retirement and begin looking to your investments to generate a specific amount of money, you might want to include more bonds and income stocks in your portfolio. But I'd suggest young boomers like yourselves need to concentrate on the stock market."

"Right, things are going to be changing dramatically because of the tidal wave of savings poised to hit the markets," Pieter said.

"By George, I think you've got it!" Hazen laughed. "As a nation, we are aging rapidly, leaving the ranks of young countries and moving into those of older ones. But keep in mind that the boom is not old, it's just hitting middle age, its big investing years. So it makes sense to see what older countries have experienced in their financial markets. I always like to use Japan as an example. For twenty years after the Second World War, Japan had a relatively low birth rate—no baby boom. As a result, they experienced an aging population in the 1970s and 1980s and—guess what—their stock markets went through the roof during that time. Here, we're just on the verge of moving into the position that Japan was in two decades ago, and I'm betting the same thing will happen to our stock markets. Japan's birth rate started into decline in the mid-1940s, and stock markets took off in the 1970s and 1980s, a lag of thirty years. Our birth rate started falling in the mid-1960s. That means we're looking for our stock market to skyrocket in the 1990s and 2000s. So far the boomers are turning up on cue."

"I'm not following you," Pieter said. "I'd always been told that Japan is a very different country than America —culturally, socially, economically."

"Right. There are big differences between the two countries. Okay, let's start from the beginning. In any country you care to look at, the average person can pick from three basic asset classes: real estate, fixed-term investments (including CDs or bonds), and then there are stocks. Some unusual events took place in Japan in the 1970s and 1980s because of that country's aging population. The Nikkei, their main stock exchange, was at a level of about 1,000 in the mid-1960s. Investors faced very low interest rates and real estate that had been priced out of sight. Sound familiar?"

"Sounds similar to the current situation here," I said. "But, Hazen, there's one thing I don't understand about the stock markets. People are always talking about the Dow breaking through 8,000. What do they mean?"

"They're talking about an index," Hazen replied. "It's a statistical tool that's used to measure the performance of the markets. In the case of the stock market, it's based on the performance of a collection of stocks and gives an overview of how the market is behaving. We look to the Dow Jones Industrial Average, which is made up of the stocks of thirty large companies listed on the stock exchange. Standard & Poor's Index of 500 Stocks—you've heard of the 'S&P 500'—is another important index. Indices have been called indicators that isolate daily ripples from the waves and the waves from the tide."

"That's a poetic analysis," I said.

"There should be room for a bit of poetry in this pursuit. After all, this stuff can get a little dry," Hazen said. "Now back to Japan. The Nikkei was sitting at about 1,000 in the mid-1960s and investors faced low interest rates and unaffordable real estate. Historically, the Japanese have been very good savers, with a savings rate well over 10 percent of their disposable household incomes. The combination of low rates and high real estate prices forced the Japanese to invest their savings in the stock market. The market was the only game in their town. Over the next twenty-odd years, beginning in the late 1960s, Japanese investors bid the index up to 39,000. To give some perspective, over the same period, the Dow Jones Industrial Average in New York moved from roughly 1,000 to 3,000. Now think about it. Why would the Japanese market outperform the U.S. market by a margin of over ten to one?"

"My guess would be it has something to do with demographics," I volunteered, grinning.

Hazen chuckled. "Good start. Many pundits, however, would suggest it was simply because the Japanese economy had so dramatically outperformed the North American economy. But I think this is far too simple an answer. I think the stock market performance was in part driven by Japanese consumers who had no other option but to invest their savings in the markets. Another very odd thing happened in Japan. In 1989, the Nikkei peaked at 39,000 when their economy was worth $2.8 trillion. By 1994, their economy had grown to $4.2 trillion, and yet their stock market had plunged to a level of 17,000. That's nothing short of bizarre, right?"

Without waiting for an answer, Hazen plunged on. "As you two continue your reading, you will discover that stock markets generally reflect the value of the economy. That's not surprising—stocks are a measure of the companies fueling the economy. Well, that's not how it panned out in Japan. An aging population caused an unusually large demand for stocks. American analysts should pay attention to this phenomenon. Unusual things are beginning to happen to our stock market, courtesy of the boomers—the kind of 'unpredictable' things that happened to the real estate market when the boomers hit it. I'd suggest that these phenomena are perfectly predictable—if you keep sight of the boom. Similarly, the ultimate decline of the Japanese market was predictable. The reason the market declined must be that, in reality, it was never worth 39,000. An aging population had bid it up."

It was pretty clear where this was going. I filled the wine glasses and passed the tray of appetizers. "So now we're at the stage where we have an aging population, and investment opportunities are limited. That means we will begin putting pressure on the markets," I said.

"Precisely. And it's already started to happen. Just look at mutual funds. Since 1990, the amount of cash and assets held in mutual funds has increased fivefold. No small potatoes. But these changes are not surprising when you consider the run-up in the stock market, the increasing number of mutual funds available, and the marketing that's promoted these funds. Our stock markets are beginning to resemble the Japanese stock market of twenty years ago."

"If this is only the beginning," Pieter said, "isn't it possible that the market could become overheated, stocks overvalued? I've been reading about price-earnings ratios, and it seems to me that a stock's price can only go so high. When stocks get overvalued, that's when a crash could occur. What is it that stock traders say—'Trees don't grow to the sky'? Plus, you've raised the story of Japan. The boom of their stock market was limited, falling back to lower levels once the 1980s were finished."

"Aha! You have been reading and those are astute questions. You've actually raised two issues—corrections in the marketplace while the boomers are the main players and the effect on the stock market of the end of the boom. First, I'll deal with your concerns about overvaluation. You know that the price-earnings ratio is the price of a stock's market price divided by its annual earnings per share. The P-E ratio is a standard measure of a stock's value. Typically, analysts say that the lower the P-E, the better. The price-earnings ratio is just one of a collection of tools analysts use to measure the potential of a stock. Well, I think the analysts are going to have to radically change their thinking on how they judge stocks, starting with the traditional view on the P-E ratio. They must adapt their thinking to the new realities that the boom will bring to the stock market. If they don't get in the game, they'll run the risk of turning into economists, and we all know how wrong they can be."

"Hazen, you've really got it in for economists," Pieter shot back.

"You're right. I digress. Let's look at P-E ratios. Why don't we use IBM's stock as an example of why I think it's time to reevaluate our reliance on these tools. IBM stock generally trades at eighteen times earnings. That translates into a P-E ratio of 18. In the future, that ratio could easily double as the boomers hit the market, causing analysts to cry that IBM stock is overpriced. But what they've got to realize is that the market has never before been subject to the kind of demand that the boomers will place on it. As the boomers hit the stock market—just like when they hit the school system and the real estate market—there is simply not going to be enough supply to go around. And that's going to bid the prices of stocks up. Here's another tidbit to chew on. In this country, the stock of telephone companies trades at an average P-E ratio that is upwards of 15. Nippon Telephone, Japan's telephone company, trades at a P-E ratio several times higher than that."

"But I still don't understand. Isn't there some bottom line where stocks are overpriced and overvalued?" I asked.

"I'm suggesting that our notion of what is overvalued will have to change. Let's go back to Japan for a minute. Their phone company regularly trades at fifty times earnings, and nobody argues that it is overvalued," said Hazen. "Let me draw a comparison. Many older Americans saw the value of their homes increase tenfold during the time they were homeowners. No one seemed to think that commodity was overpriced during its run-up in value. If there's a demand for a product and that product is in short supply, the price will go up. Guaranteed."

Just as Hazen finished his sentence, a bell sounded in his kitchen.

"Perfect timing. Just as I finished telling you about the indirect impact boomers will have on the stock market, my oven tells me that our lasagna is ready. We can talk over dinner about the direct effects the boomers have brought and continue to bring to the market," he said, leading us into the kitchen. He quickly doled out the chores—Pieter set to tossing a salad; I began slicing a crusty loaf of fresh bread.

—

As we sat down to steaming plates filled with Hazen's famous (self-proclaimed) lasagna, our host started off again. "So far we've addressed only one way in which boomers will affect the stock market—by pouring their retirement savings into it. But let's not forget that you've been directly affecting the market for years—ever since you were born, in fact. Your mere presence has caused fortunes to be made on the stock market."

"That's quite a claim," I said.

"And it's true. By affecting trends and consumption, boomers have been the bread and butter of many companies, creating profits and pushing stock prices up. Do you think McDonald's would have grown to the size it is without the boom pushing it along? And why do you think they're trying to make their menu more grown-up by introducing things like the Crispy Chicken Deluxe and the Arch Deluxe? McDonald's executives are watching boomers and their kids—the echo boomers—grow up, and they don't want to be left behind. And how about Disney? You grew up with Mickey, Donald, and the rest of the gang. Now it's Bill Gates's turn. Do you think he would have done as well marketing software to a tiny generation? You folks are the ultimate impact players. You hit products hard and cause great opportunities for companies and their shareholders. You even helped to save Chrysler," he added.

"Right. I remember that story," Pieter said.

"Then you recall that a decade after Congress stepped in and saved their bacon, the boom decided that their products are magic, especially their minivan—*once* the boomer vehicle of choice to move around their precious broods. And guess what? Chrysler's profits became magic. Sales continue to be very solid—not surprising when you consider that minivans account for almost one quarter of their sales. That has had a big effect on the company's share prices—they grew by a healthy 34 percent through 1996 and into 1997. But for that 'magic wagon,' Chrysler, along with Studebaker, would have been a footnote in car-making history. The boom can congratulate itself for helping to build Chrysler to the industry leader it is today. But Chrysler can't rest on its laurels. The boomers are aging, and so are their kids. If Chrysler wants to keep its winning streak going, it better change gears and head full speed into the sport utility market because that's were the boomers are headed."

I laughed. "Boomers rule, as our skateboarding son would say."

"There's another expression I wouldn't mind stealing— I mean borrowing," Hazen quipped.

"Just as long as you pay him a royalty in the form of financial advice," I lobbed back.

"It's a deal," Hazen said. "But back to cars. The other car companies were slower off the mark than Chrysler, but they too have now got it figured out: boomers rule. There's still plenty of life left in the minivan market, and General Motors is desperately trying to squeeze into it, grasping for a piece of the lucrative boomer pie. GM spent several hundred million dollars to move a re-designed minivan onto dealers' lots in time for the 1997 model year. Boomers are definitely driving this market. And they'll stay at the wheel for a long time to come. By 2030, there'll be 32 million Americans over seventy-five, and plenty will still be motoring around. Who knows, GM might oust Chrysler yet. By then the boomers will have permanently parked both their minivans and sport utes and be well into their Cadillac years."

"And Gerber was one of the first to catch the wave, right?" said Pieter.

"Right," Hazen replied. "And there have been plenty of companies since then. Look at Nike targeting forty-year-old women. 'Just beginning to go' is one of their slogans. That's exactly the kind of upbeat message an aging boomer wants to hear. I guarantee that will sell Nikes to boomer women who participate in the silly walk."

"That's called power walking, Hazen," I said.

"Whatever. It sure does look silly to me. But it certainly doesn't look silly to Reebok. Reebok owns Rock-port, a company famous for its walking shoes. Who is its target audience? The boomers, of course. Rockport, real-izing it wants to tap into the largest and most prosperous market in the world now, has come up with an advertising slogan—the 'New Comfort Attitude,' aimed at telling consumers that it can sell them shoes that will make their lives more comfortable, more productive, and more adventurous. Those are all messages boomers love to hear. Next—how about Tums? We grew up thinking it was for upset tummies. Now we learn it's a great calcium supplement. Coincidence? I think not. Just a savvy manufacturer looking at a huge aging market concerned with the possibility of brittle bones."

"From what you're saying," I said, "it should be a great time for companies who cater to the needs of an older population, especially a group like the boomers who are so concerned with their appearance and health."

"Assuming the company is well managed and has a product that boomers want or need, the sky's the limit. Let me give you a couple of really diverse examples to illustrate the breadth of boomer power."

"Shoot," Pieter said.

"Gardening. Harley-Davidsons. Meals in a can. Estée Lauder makeup."

I laughed. "That's a pretty weird list of stuff."

"Well, each has its boomer story," Hazen said. "Let's start our engines with the Harleys. Even though boomers are starting to save, they still like to indulge their wants. And they truly want to stay young. What better way to do it than by fulfilling a lifelong dream and riding a hog? The company can't keep up with demand. Look, they've even got that fancy store selling Harley gear on upscale Newbury Street downtown. And I'd point out that the average age of a Harley purchaser is forty-plus."

"It's not how I would spend my money," I said, "but your point is well taken. Think about what boomers really want to own."

"That's one thing to keep in mind. Here's another. Think about how they spend their time. The kids are getting older and boomers are blooming. And I mean that literally. Gardening has become an increasingly popular hobby in North America. Hank loves you folks. If you need proof of that, visit your neighborhood newsstand and you'll find a healthy crop of gardening magazines. It's a strong corner of the magazine industry. It's estimated that, each year, Americans are increasing the amount they spend on their lawns and gardens by about 10 percent. Not peanuts, I'd say."

"Speaking of peanuts, don't you have demographic stats on that topic?" Pieter joked.

"Like I've said before, demographics doesn't explain everything. For example, haven't you ever wondered why it takes three cans of water for orange juice and four for lemonade? A mystery never fully explained. Speaking of cans, next on the agenda: meals in a can. Here's a product that's got a future, although it's not quite as much fun as gardening. These nutritional drinks, like Ensure and Boost, are touted as the drink of an older generation. And that's where we are headed. Companies that once marketed baby formula are seeing where the consumers are heading, and they are following by producing a drink loaded with vitamins and minerals that appeals to folks who don't have the time or ability to eat properly. Of course, they're appealing to the health-conscious boomer. Any company that can tap into the health worries of the boomers will land a guaranteed and large market."

"I'd agree with that," Pieter said. "Health becomes a pretty high priority as you age. Look at all the healthy stuff they sell down at Jera's Juice on Harvard Street—every vitamin you'd ever want, and they don't use frozen orange juice. It's always packed in there."

"But don't forget this is the boom you're talking about. They not only want to feel good; they want to look good. That brings me to Estée Lauder. I've just done some research on this cosmetics company because it went public and listed shares on the New York Stock Exchange in late 1995. They're very clever marketers who have paid plenty of attention to the women now purchasing their products. They know what concerns boomer women. And so far their strategy appears to be working. Their stock hit the market at $26 a share and, within a year, it was trading at $50. Let me see if I can remember some of the tag lines they used in their recent advertisements," Hazen said, scratching his head. "Okay, I've got it: 'Fewer visible lines now. Firmer skin in the future.' Here's another two: 'Before your skin gets a minute older,' and 'Suddenly, your skin is just not as resilient. Now we can help bring it back.' Not a bad memory for an old guy."

"Hey, it sounds good to me," I said. "I'd gladly get rid of a few wrinkles. Okay, I can add to this conversation," I continued. "I'd say you also have to pay attention to other boomer sensibilities when predicting the future."

"Like what, Meredith?" Pieter asked.

"Like Hazen suggested, boomers have a lot of the same concerns their parents did, such as health issues. But they also put their own spin on things. Ruth told me an interesting story about Anheuser-Busch. That company is attempting to profit from boomers' taste for quality as opposed to quantity. They're counting on boomers who want a higher-quality beer in moderation as opposed to a lower-quality beer in massive quantities. Capacity ain't what it used to be." We all laughed.

"That's a great example," Hazen responded. "Now you know the kind of thinking to apply when looking for companies that will profit from an aging boom. But don't forget that, although boomers are getting older, they're not yet old. Operators of long-term care facilities, like nursing and retirement centers, are often touted as boomer stocks. They may be interesting and well-managed companies, but they're not ready to be hit by the boomers. They're catering to your parents' generation. A word of caution. Don't get ahead of yourselves." Hazen reached for the salad bowl.

"Now it's my turn," he said. "I'm going to do some original boomer research. Tell me how you plan to spend the summer with the kids."

Our stock market lecture ended, and we moved into a spirited discussion of our plans for the next few months.

13

Why?

Tuesday evenings had taken
on special significance in the DeMarco household this
spring. A new family tradition had taken hold. After an
early dinner, we all walked over to the park to watch
Emily play soccer, followed by a visit to J.P.Licks, our
neighborhood ice cream parlor for a late dessert: cookies-
and-cream cones all round. Pieter was particularly enjoying this ritual. His father, born in Italy, loved soccer,
and Pieter was an avid player as a kid. These evenings
brought back good memories of similar evenings spent
with his mother and father. We felt we were all figuring
out what was really important.

As the four of us set off toward the park, Emily loaded
with soccer stuff, we spotted Hazen soaking in the daily
paper, comfortably ensconced in the lawn chair parked
on his front porch.

"Thanks for dinner and the stock market report,
Hazen," Pieter piped up, crossing the street and leaning
over Hazen's front gate. "We're coming to appreciate the

importance that our generation will have on our future well-being."

"Stock market beware: boomers on the way," Hazen replied, smiling.

Pieter said, "Your lecture has left us with a number of questions about the stock market. When you have the time, we'd like to run them by you, just to make sure we've got it right."

"Questions. The spice of life. Too many folks only want the answers. They don't even know what the questions are. I'm a great believer in understanding the why of things. If you understand why things work the way they do, then you're far better equipped to understand the answers. If you understand why the stock market will take off, you'll be in a much better position to take advantage of it." Hazen folded the newspaper in his lap. "I see you're in a bit of a hurry," he said. Emily was tugging at my sleeve.

"Care to join us?" I asked. "We're off to the park to watch Emily play soccer."

"That sounds like a great idea. It's a perfect evening for the park. There's a documentary about the 1960s that I want to watch at nine, but I've got some time. Maybe you can hit me with a few questions while we're cheering for Emily. Right, Emily? Can I help you carry some of your gear?" he asked gallantly.

"Sure," replied Emily. "My mom and dad never help me. They say, 'A girl's got to look after her own gear.'" She cast a look our way while handing Hazen her soccer shoes.

"Listen, kiddo," I said, "there'll come a time when you're going to be glad that you know how to look after yourself and your own stuff. It's all about taking respon-sibility for Emily DeMarco."

"Your mom's right, you know," Hazen said to her. "It's important to know how to look after yourself. Did you know that even your mom and dad have some things to learn? That's what I've been helping them with for the past few weeks."

Emily smiled broadly, delighted to see her dad and me tweaked by Hazen.

"See. It's never to late too learn," I said, patting her on the back.

We arrived at the park. Emily ran off to join her team-mates, and Malcolm, skateboard in hand, sauntered over to join his buddies shooting baskets on the court. Parents are not to be acknowledged when you're in high-cool mode.

"Here's a revelation for you," said Hazen. "Soccer is now one of the top participation sports for children in this country."

Pieter turned to him. "Really? But surely baseball is still the favorite."

"Nope. Soccer's beaten out baseball."

Pieter laughed. "You just can't resist a good trend, can you, Hazen?"

"This stuff sticks to my brain, I guess. Maybe that's why I've made it my life's work."

We had a few minutes before the game started so the three of us ambled over to a quiet spot at the end of the field. I jumped in with the first question.

"Hazen, you know that I'm nervous about the stock market," I said.

"I'm coming to realize that, Meredith," Hazen said with a smile.

"Well, it seems to me that all the things the boomers have hit eventually go the other way. Real estate prices went up. Then they went down. The stock market is on its way up. But when will it come down? You told us about the stock market in Japan going up and then coming down. When will that happen here?"

Hazen looked pleased with my query. "I was wondering when you'd ask me this one. In fact, I was surprised you didn't ask it at our stock market dinner. Okay, for starters, the market is going to run out of steam at some point. It's inevitable. As I always say, if you live by the boom, you die by the boom. Look what happened to some of this country's biggest real estate developers— they thought the surge in their market would never stop. But it did. So the boom will stop pressuring the stock market at some point, and the key question is when. Let's look at the stats. The oldest boomers won't be ready for retirement until the 2010s. People tend to keep accumulating net assets until their late sixties. So that pushes us out to the mid-2010s. What does this mean? The oldest boomers will start cashing in on their investments sometime around 2015."

"So the big correction will come in 2015?" Pieter inquired.

"No, I'm not saying that. Not at all. Remember, the median age of boomers is still under forty. We're not going to see boomers start to retire in big numbers until about 2020. And even then, I don't believe there will be a huge plunge in the prices of stocks. I've told you that people are predictable. Well, aging is a slow process. Retirees won't eat into all of their savings in the first year of their retirements. It will have taken them a long time to assemble their retirement investments. It will take them many years to unwind and consume those investments. The shift in demand for stocks will take place over a long period of time. In fact, I'd predict a stagnation in the prices of stocks rather than a crash. This will likely start around 2020 to 2025 when the bulk of the boom moves into retirement. We've seen similar situations where other markets have hit equilibrium—equal numbers of buyers and sellers. The result? The market treads water for a number of years."

"So you do think this stock market boom will end?" I asked.

"Of course, but don't lose sight of the big picture, Meredith. The pressure that the boom is placing on the market will end sometime. It has to. Don't forget the key demographic truth—we all die. Boomers can't last forever, no matter how much stock market investors would like them to. But the end of the boomers is a long way out, and they're going to keep pressuring the stock market well into the twenty-first century. Don't miss out on this opportunity just because things might go into decline when we hit the 2020s. And yes, in the interim, there will be corrections along the way. They've occurred in the past; they'll occur in the future. What you've got to learn is not to let these corrections shake you out of the market. There's more I want to tell you about this, but I think I'll save it until our mutual funds lecture. Remind me that I want to return to this topic."

I said, "Okay, so you're telling me I've got at least twenty good years of investing in the stock market ahead of me and that I shouldn't worry?"

"Yes and no," Hazen answered, smiling. "Yes, I am saying that you have at least twenty good years to invest in the market. I'm not alone in my thinking on this. *Kiplinger's* recently included an article on the topic. Like me, they predicted that the market will stay favorable for many years. The worst-case scenario is a future market that delivers sub-par performance. And no, I think you have lots to worry about. It's in your nature to worry, Meredith. What I'm urging you to do is to keep an open mind. Look long and hard at what's going on around you. Read and think. The key is believing in the boomer impact. And stick to your long-term plan. Don't get shaken out by short-term corrections." He leaned up against a large maple tree.

"One more thing I should add," he continued, "don't underestimate the power of the generation following the boom. I think I already mentioned to you that many of them are thinking about saving for retirement—already. And if there is a partial privatization of Social Security— like many are thinking will occur—that will certainly create a new demand for stocks. And the big buyers will be the members of that generation."

"Now it's my turn," Pieter said. "When the boom hit other commodities—schools, real estate, money markets —there was an initial shortage of the commodity. Then, over the years, supply catches up with demand. Wouldn't it be easy for the financial markets to simply create more stock to satisfy the demand the boomers will put on this commodity?"

Hazen watched the kids pile onto the field. "That's another great question. You two are really doing your homework. Many of us look at a paper stock certificate and assume it's easy for a company to produce as much stock as it would like. In fact, that notion couldn't be further from the truth. First, let's look at companies that are already listed on the stock market. Stocks represent the real value of a company. New shares would be offered only if the company needed to finance additional business requirements, not because the demand for their stocks had increased. Now, think about why companies issue shares in the first place. A share issue is a way to raise money. I would suggest that over the next twenty years, companies that need capital are going to be looking at borrowing money rather than raising cash via a stock issue."

"Why would you say that?" I asked.

"Remember what I said about the long-term outlook for interest rates?"

"Right, you said rates would stay low for years to come," I responded.

"Well, companies have a duty to their shareholders to run their businesses properly. That means raising money as cheaply as possible. I'd suggest that given long-term low interest rates, the cheapest way for a company to raise money will be to borrow it. Share issues simply won't be an attractive alternative for many companies," Hazen concluded.

"But what about companies that aren't yet listed on the markets? Won't new companies start up and see the stock market as a viable way of raising cash?" asked Pieter.

"Good, you've introduced my second point—new companies. Ideally, over the next twenty years, plenty of new companies will start up. That will be great for the economy. But it's not as easy to start a company and take it public as it is to, say, build a subdivision. Stock isn't just a piece of paper. It takes years of hard work and planning, plus a healthy helping of luck, to nurture a successful business. Real estate developers took a full twenty years to catch up to the demand boomers put on the housing market. While they were trying to catch up, the pressure built and the prices of existing houses soared. Now, when these developers were operating at peak capacity, it might have taken only two to three years to build a subdivision. But it generally takes much longer than that for a company to get up and running and issue a successful IPO."

"What's an IPO?" I asked.

"That's the initial public offering—the first time a company issues shares to the public. It could easily take upwards of ten years for a new firm to get to that stage. Here's a good example—I'm sure you've heard of Ralph Lauren. Ralph Lauren started selling ties under the Polo name back in 1967, but its IPO—a very successful one, I might add—didn't happen until 1997. Good quality stocks won't be created quickly enough to satisfy demand. A word of caution—as the stock market continues to rise, we're going to see companies scurrying to file

IPOs. Beware of companies that can't back up promise with performance. Look for IPOs from solid companies. It's going to be interesting to watch," said Hazen. "In fact, amazing though it sounds, some analysts are arguing that the supply of stocks in the market could shrink. Certain companies with excess profits are buying back their shares these days. Mergers, acquisitions, and takeovers will also reduce the stock on the markets. These trends by themselves could cause share prices to rise."

"Here's another one for you, Hazen," Pieter said. "I know you keep talking about boomers hitting the stock markets, but I recently read an article that said the institutions are the real power behind the markets these days."

"Pete, I'll get you a copy of a recent *Federal Reserve Bulletin* that reported the percentage of families owning publicly traded shares has recently fallen for most demographic groups. Institutions hold a greater chunk of the market—an ever-increasing piece of the stock market pie. But don't be misled by that data," Hazen said.

"It seems to me that either institutions dominate the market or they don't. Isn't it that simple?" Pieter asked.

"Look out at the soccer field and tell me what you see," Hazen replied. The game had just begun; every kid on the field was chasing the ball. Lots of offense, no defense. No score. In fact, well into the season, Emily's team had yet to score. I waved to Emily, who stopped chasing the ball for a moment to return the greeting.

"I don't know, Hazen. It looks like a bunch of kids crowded around a ball," I replied.

"Exactly. The herd mentality. Just like the boomers. I saw Emily's coach reviewing passing techniques and positional play before the game, but when you let them loose on the field, they all just chase the ball. You could throw a blanket over them. When your generation moves at anything, it looks like the same game. You crowd around the commodity. You are rushing at the stock market, but you're doing it through institutions."

"How can an individual hit the stock market through an institution?" I asked.

"First and foremost, think mutual funds," Hazen explained. "Then add trust and insurance companies, banks, and pension funds to the mix. These are the big institutional investors in the market, and they're all funded by individuals like you. As boomers start to save, money is building up in these institutions and, as a result, putting unprecedented pressure on the markets. Some of this pressure is structural, and this is going to make it hard for the bears to slow this bull market down. Short-term bad news will have an effect, but the longer trend will ultimately carry the day because the boomers themselves are a long-term trend—a generation that stretches for two decades."

"When you mention structural pressures, what do you mean?" I asked.

"Yes, that confused me as well," added Pieter.

"Well, many of these institutions have been encouraging their clients to purchase products—be it life insurance, mutual funds, whatever—on a regular basis, usually monthly. The purchases occur automatically, courtesy of pre-authorized payment agreements. Pensions have worked that way for years. Huge amounts of money roll into the markets automatically, and regularly. As boomers age, they can afford to put more and more money into these investments, and the asset values hitting the stock market are just going to keep on going up and up. Lately, the boomers have started to pick up two critical themes: pay yourself first, and practice dollar-cost averaging, a fancy way of saying that you invest regularly, usually monthly. Saving on a regular basis has automatically put pressure on the markets as boomers have turned more and more to equity mutual funds.

"Here's an interesting statistic about a fine Boston firm. Fidelity Investments, the mutual fund giant that *Fortune* magazine suggests is the most dominant financial services institution in the world, has about half its assets under management in retirement money, including 401(k) and IRA accounts. That means this money keeps rolling in automatically—every month. And that brings up another important element to consider. As I've already said, once investors set up these monthly investment plans, they run automatically. What does this mean? It means that these plans don't think. The money continually flows in and continues its pressure on the supply of stocks, increasing the prices—no matter what twists and turns the market might take."

I watched Pieter as he stood quietly, absorbing this information. Suddenly, the soccer ball flew down to our end of the field.

"Run, Emily!" Pieter shouted, seeing her leading the herd down the field. The three of us retreated behind the maple tree to avoid being trampled by the pack of kids.

"Here's another question," Pieter began, as the players ran back up the field. "What about the old adage 'buy low, sell high'? I've been reading articles about this bull market that question how much bull is left. It seems to me that markets are priced extremely high these days. Doesn't that mean this is a poor time to buy?"

"I've been waiting for this one. You're quite right. When prices are high, don't buy. But I want to tell you about a specific date—July 8, 1932," Hazen replied.

"Sounds like this could be a Depression story," I said.

"Well, sort of," Hazen said slowly. "That's the day the Dow Jones Average hit its century low of 40. That's four zero—40. But it's moved to a level over 8,000. The boomers' parents were alive for this incredible increase, but many advised their kids to steer clear of the market, Meredith. What I'm saying is that for some folks the emotional price of the market is always too high, so they avoid it. Is the market high today? Well, compared to 1932, it sure is. But I believe this market is going to go a lot higher because the boom has shown up.

"If you're planning a long-term accumulation of quality stocks and mutual funds, the best time to buy is right now. Don't forget that we've come out of a decade when stocks underperformed both bonds and real estate. That's very unusual. No surprise, however. The boomers were pressuring interest rates and buying real estate. Guess what? Retirement is now front and center in the minds of the boomers and the stock market is suddenly looking very boomer-friendly. It's become the best game in town. It's funny, but so many people started to believe that the way things were in the 1970s and 1980s, with high interest rates and soaring real estate prices, was the way the world was going to stay. They let the boom skew their view. It turns out that the boomers were responsible for the trends of those decades. And now the boom has turned its attention elsewhere."

Just as Hazen finished his response, Emily broke into the clear with the ball and drove it just wide of her own net. After the excitement died down, we went back to our question-and-answer session.

"Hazen, Pieter and I have been watching the media since you introduced us to these ideas. We've seen numerous articles about how great the economy is doing now. But the media is still full of plenty of things that concern us. You know, things like the government debt, job losses, business failures, bankruptcies. It has a way of working on you, worrying you. We can't help but feel that the good times aren't here to stay. And if that's the case, how can our stock market continue to perform well?"

"This issue of the media affects the anxiety that many of us bring to the stock markets," Hazen replied. "Boomers are well educated and, as a result, many are news junkies. It's always important to remember that different groups have their own agendas. The news media are no different. They're in the business of selling the news. News, by definition, tends to focus on the short term. The boomers are not news—you're a long-term trend. You've been sitting in the economy for the past fifty years and you've got another fifty to go. What you've got to keep in mind is the overriding effect that boomers will continue to have on any news that you hear. The boom exerts a powerful influence over many, many things that happen.

"Let me give you an example. There is a lot of media coverage concerning government debt levels in this country. Right now, that's news. Why is that? How did the boomers influence this news story? I'd suggest that their very size is setting the national agenda. Now that they're the major taxpayers—the mainstream of the economy—they want the debt dealt with."

"We talked about this when you lectured us on interest rates. You suggested that boomers' savings will make the government debt a non-issue," Pieter answered.

"Exactly. Combined with the policies that the boomers want to see in place, the very existence of the boom can overpower many short-term bad news items," Hazen concluded, turning to watch the action on the field.

I said to Pieter, "We should ask Hazen about the statistics you read about the money boomers are about to inherit."

"Oh, right. I read an article that said boomers are poised to inherit more than 10 trillion dollars from their parents over the next several decades. Meredith and I were amused by that number. We're certainly not part of that lucky group. But surely that huge transfer of wealth will have an effect on the markets?" Pieter said.

"Actually, Pieter, I think it will affect several markets. First, let's see where that money is now and why. I mentioned to you that your parents' generation was quite fortunate. The boomers bid up the prices of their homes and the interest rates they received at the banks during their prime saving years. This inevitably created our first generation to retire wealthy. And that explains the size of this potential inheritance. Now, where is this money? Well, lots of it is still sitting in real estate or at the bank. Courtesy of the boomers, this was a wise financial strategy over the past couple of decades. When your generation begins to inherit their parents' homes, they're not going to keep them as shrines to their memories. Nope, those houses are going to be sold. Now, keep in mind, we tend to inherit, on average, in our late forties. Generally, mortgages are paid off by then or greatly reduced. The boomers are going to be looking to invest that cash, along with the money their parents have sitting at the bank."

"I think I know where this is headed," Pieter piped up.

"First off, it's going to pay down debts and then what's left will go into savings for retirement," Hazen said. "I think an awful lot of this inheritance is going to flow into retirement accounts."

Pieter smiled. "Now I know for certain where this is headed."

"So tell us, smart guy," said Hazen, returning Pieter's smile.

"Once the boomers pay their debts, the balance of the money will head to IRAs and 401(k)s. Because boomers are in their prime saving years and interest rates are stuck at a low point, the majority of this money will head into mutual funds or stocks—or both. How's that?"

"And who says hi-tech guys can't function in the real world? Bravo, Pieter. You're all set. One last discussion on the intricacies of the mutual fund market and I think we're done," said Hazen, looking pleased.

"Hazen, we've already spoken to a couple of investment types and a lot of numbers have come up. How much do you think Pieter and I should try to accumulate for our retirement?" I asked.

"Meredith, this is one question I can't answer for you," Hazen said. "That's not what I do. You've got to figure out that number yourself. But a good financial adviser will be able to help you. No, I'm here to give you the big picture: the why of investing your money. I want you to have the big, long-term picture firmly in your heads before you get down to the nitty-gritty of saving and investing. Having a solid working knowledge of where the boom is headed will make your gut reactions much more astute. It's always worked for me."

The game was winding down. Eight players remained on the field. Six were sitting on the sidelines watching the action. The rest had migrated over to the swing set and the teeter-totter. Emily's team came out of the game with their perfect record intact—four scoreless ties. We gestured to Malcolm to gather his stuff. Off we wandered—the four of us—to the highlight of the evening—ice cream cones at J.P.Licks. Hazen waved goodbye, heading home to relive the 1960s.

14

Getting It Together

"Here's what I want to know. Why are you and I doing this? Why aren't Hazen and Pieter organizing who-takes-what for the weekend away at your cottage?" Ruth asked. We both looked at one another and shrugged. Ruth locked the office door behind her, bidding Mr. Garcia goodbye as we started off toward the cafeteria.

Pieter and I had invited Ruth to join Hazen and our family for the first summer weekend at our place on Spofford Lake. It was our way of saying thank you to the both of them for everything they'd done for us over the spring and to celebrate the blossoming of our relationships into firm friendships. Pieter hadn't had the opportunity to get to know Ruth, so we decided that sharing a weekend would rectify that situation. All that needed to be done was the planning. And opening a cottage is somewhat akin to undertaking a military invasion—lots to think about—and this is one attack where you can't just sneak up on the enemy.

Ruth was right, I thought as we walked down the hall. Since I'd started working for her, I'd been struggling with a distinct lack of time, grateful to Pieter for helping me by cleaning toilet bowls and peeling potatoes, but resentful that I still had complete responsibility for organizing the family, the house, and the cottage. Pieter would gladly run out for a jug of milk on a Sunday evening, but it was up to me to keep track of things and realize we'd need it for Monday's breakfast.

"You're right, I could use some help," I said to Ruth as we entered the cafeteria.

"If it's any consolation, you're not alone," Ruth answered. "The vast majority of women with children still at home are in the labor force. But even though they're out there in the trenches every day, most mothers in families where both spouses work—like yours—still carry the major responsibility for child care and household chores. Double whammy! It's estimated that women do nearly two-thirds of the unpaid work in this country. It's still a bit of an uphill battle."

"Okay, so here's the deal," I whispered conspiratorially to Ruth as we carried our trays through the cafeteria, checking out the day's offerings. "We'll organize and figure what needs to be done, then we'll give the guys all the chores."

"Meredith, I like your style!" Ruth threw her head back and laughed heartily. We both settled on the chicken salad and began our search for a table.

"Seriously, though," Ruth continued, settling into her seat. "I've been really impressed watching you fit yourself into the work world. Do you remember the first day I met you, when you came into my office looking for a job and I called you a domestic feminist?"

I nodded. "I've thought about that phrase," I said, "and I'd like to amend it to 'family feminist.' Domestic makes it sound as if I'm locked in the kitchen. But you're right, I'm committed to the notion that women have the right to choose what's right for them, but first and foremost, I'm committed to my family. The welfare of my children is my highest concern, my biggest responsibility, my top priority."

"It's a funny thing about growing up. You grow up," replied Ruth slowly.

"How do you mean?"

"I'm talking about the emotional and spiritual aspects of growing up. Adults should be more mature, more responsible than the children they all once were. A mensch, as my uncle would say. That's a Yiddish word for a person of integrity and honor. But you don't become a mensch without some work. It's always easier to shirk your obligations. Interestingly, studies show that you're not unlike the rest of your generation. Both men and women are placing the needs of their families ahead of career advancement. They're growing up. Society is maturing, and it's not simply an age thing."

"No kidding," I replied. "Nobody prepared me for this family thing. You don't really have a clue how much love you will have for your children. On the downside, before kids arrive on the scene, you have absolutely no appreciation of how much work they'll be."

"It's been particularly difficult for you boomers, not that I feel real sorry for you," said Ruth. "Think about what the 1960s were all about: personal freedom and experimentation. The individual was the focal point of the generation. Boomer demographics was right for that view of the world—so many of you, so young, so foot-loose. The first cohort of boomers were young and bumming through life in a beat-up Volkswagen Beetle. That was far preferable to settling down to a job, family, commitments, and obligations at an early age. Who needed others when you could devote yourself to you?"

"But that approach is so shortsighted," I replied. "Focus too long on yourself and you become pretty lonely. Life doesn't have a lot of meaning."

"Exactly. We're not meant to be a collection of Robinson Crusoes. We're social animals. But the technology unleashed by you boomers has made it ever more difficult to fulfill our social roles. Think about how many hours people spend in front of the television or computer screen or on the telephone," she continued. "Those are hours not spent face-to-face with human beings, being human. Then layer on all the social changes that have occurred in the past forty years—women are better educated, people are older when they get married, more women are out in the work force, more one-parent families, higher divorce rates, people moving around the country. Not all of that change is bad. I'd suggest that much of it is extremely good. And don't get me wrong—I'm certainly not advocating a return to the old days of no television and Mrs. Cleaver at home in the kitchen. But it's no longer quite so easy to be part of a community as it once was.

"Yet that doesn't mean that we have lost our need to be part of a community to fill our emotional and spiritual needs. In fact, while attendance at religious services has been dropping for some time, there has been a dramatic increase in Americans' interest in spirituality. Staying connected is just harder to do these days. It's harder to find the time, harder to maintain connections when families and friends are spread across the country. It's critical to find and focus on a community rather than live as a collection of unconnected individuals. I see you and Pieter working away at establishing a community for your family. And I'm optimistic that lots of other boomers are growing up and taking their responsibilities to family and community seriously. The statistics bear out my optimism. Boomers are placing greater value than ever on traits like honesty, kindness, politeness, forgiveness, and generosity. As they grow older they share more and more of the values of their parents. Kind of scary, isn't it? Becoming your parents . . . "

"What are Pieter and I doing to promote this community thing?" I asked.

"Look at this weekend you're organizing. It sure would be easier for you to hang out in the city. There'd be no extra shopping, nothing to organize. Instead, not only are you packing up your kids, but you're inviting Hazen and me along for the ride. It may just seem like a fun weekend to you, but you're sending a loud, clear message to your kids."

"Ruth, it's just a family getaway to the cottage."

"Yes, it's that too. But sometimes we get so lost in our daily routines, rushing through life at top speed, worrying about whether we have milk for breakfast, that we don't take the time to look at the bigger picture. For your family, this weekend is part of the bigger picture of family life—being together with people you love, having fun, enjoying a traditional American experience. Look, you're sending important messages of trust, stability, security, constancy, and intimacy. I'd say you and Pieter have developed a life plan—by default. Maybe you've never sat down and consciously thought about it, but I'd say that you have created a life plan for yourself."

"You're sounding like Hazen—again. He's always talking to us about creating our financial plan."

"Putting a financial plan in place is an integral part of a life plan. You have to have money to live your life and take care of your needs and those of your family. A life plan is all about making choices for yourself, setting out a framework that defines your life."

"Sounds far too organized for me," I said.

"Hey, you're looking at the Queen of Disorganization! You've seen the disaster zone that I call an office. You should see the inside of my kitchen cupboards. You'd call the health department!" We both laughed.

"If you're the Queen, then I'm your Princess of Clutter," I answered.

"But that mess is one small part of my life plan," Ruth said. "I decided a long time ago that there were more important things for me to be doing than tidying cupboards. It's just not important to me."

"So what is important?"

"Well, everybody's different, so everybody's plan will be different. What's important to you may not be important to me. I'm certainly not suggesting that you sit down at your computer and draw up a family constitution. But I am saying it's an extremely worthwhile exercise to sit down and discuss where you'd like to take your lives. I look at my plan as my own personal moral code. The foundation of my code is ever so basic—treat others as you would be treated. I learned this at my uncle's knee and have never forgotten it. Here, I'll give you two examples of key components of my plan.

"Number one: since his birth, Dylan has been my top priority. And I always wanted him to feel part of an extended family, to be there for family celebrations, both happy and sad. That's one of the reasons I've stayed in Boston all these years—it's close to my family in New York. I maybe could have progressed further in my career if I'd gone somewhere else, but that wasn't in my life plan. Number two: I work hard, I save, and I plan. I have to look after my finances because I don't want to be financially reliant on anyone else. I value my independence, and I want to live at a certain standard."

"Ruth, the day you hired me, you spoke in almost mystical terms about the coincidence of my arriving on your doorstep the day you needed help. You said coincidences happened when you needed them. Synchronicity, you called it. How does all that fit in with this life plan stuff? If you've got everything planned out, where do coincidences fit in?"

Ruth laughed her long throaty chuckle. "Life isn't always going to conform to your personal plan. As you know, life's got more than a few tricks up her sleeve. You boomers have been a bit late learning that lesson. Unlike the generations that preceded you, the folks who grew up in the Depression years and endured war, you've had a pretty easy go of life. Till now. And here we are with an entire huge generation poised on the cusp of a mid-life crisis. Things can get tough at mid-life—health issues, work issues, kid issues. Worst of all, your body's started to give out. You need glasses, you've got gray hairs, your joints ache. You can't delude yourself into thinking you're still twenty-one."

"Aha, you noticed my new reading glasses," I said. "I still can't believe I need them."

"Then you know what I'm talking about. But you can prepare yourself for those tricks of life if you've thought out where you want to go and how you want to get there. I remember talking to you about Dylan's unexpected arrival. I certainly wasn't planning on becoming a mother. I had my sights set on becoming a world-famous sociologist. 'When you look to the heights, hang on to your hat' is one of my uncle's favorite warnings. Sure enough, life sent me Dylan and everything changed. But part of my plan was to stay connected to my family. I took one look at Dylan and my notion of family blossomed. The details of my plan have changed over time, but the fundamentals have always stayed the same."

"But, Ruth, not everyone has your strength or ability."

"You're right. I've been lucky. But everyone can give some thought to how they'd like to live their lives. It's funny how luck dispenses its favors. Hazen once told me about this golfer, Lee Trevino, who said, 'The more I practice, the luckier I get.' It's amazing how much of life is about choices. We choose how we want to treat our children, our friends, our lovers. How they treat us is in large measure based on how we treat them. So it's a combination of circularity and synchronicity, I guess."

She laughed. "What is it with us, Meredith? Whenever we get talking, we end up solving the problems of the world."

I could tell my wise woman had ended her philosophizing for the day. "I guess our biggest problem right now is figuring out who's going to bring dinner for Saturday night at the cottage."

Ruth hauled a pad of paper out of her backpack and we set to making lists divvying up the work—between the four of us.

15

Mutual Experiences

It had been a good meeting. Pieter and I spent late Friday afternoon doing our "homework": meeting with an investment adviser.

We had taken the advice of our friends Heather and Tom, consulting their adviser, who was with a large downtown brokerage firm. He reviewed ideas on how to set up a plan. Interestingly, we'd heard quite a bit of it before—from Hazen. We went through the concept of paying ourselves first. The broker suggested that money should be withdrawn automatically from our checking account at the beginning of each month. He pointed out that this should be done within our IRAs to maximize our tax deductions. By doing this, he explained, it would be easier on our cash flow and we'd average out our purchasing power through the year.

We also discussed our retirement needs. He provided some projections of the amount we'd need to be saving to meet those needs. He reviewed the types of investments that he felt were best for us at this time, providing us with some background material to review, including some brochures and prospectuses from mutual fund companies. Like Hazen, he was adamant that we know what we'd be buying into, explaining that mutual funds varied widely in content, focus, and sales charges. Although we also discussed investing in some blue chip stocks, the broker suggested that we stick to mutual funds for now, given the relatively modest amounts we were going to commit to our saving plan.

We broached the subject of the children's education, and he suggested monthly deposits into a mutual fund. He had a great line about finances that hit home with both of us: "This stuff isn't really all that easy to understand, so the best way to stay ahead of it is not to make it any more complicated than necessary." You know, keep it simple. Mutual funds fit that bill for a wide variety of consumers.

But mostly we just chatted, trying to get a feel for this individual, determining whether we felt we could trust him, whether he had an understanding of our personalities and our needs. He brought up the subject of his fees, outlining the services we could expect from him. He raised the issue of the thousands of investing possibilities offered by the markets, explaining that he could give a professional opinion on what would be right for us. He outlined the difficulties in deciding which mutual fund to purchase equipped only with information concerning the past performance of funds—and produced a study demonstrating that the investments of people who availed themselves of professional advice have generally outperformed the average deposit-based investor dealing with the local bank or trust company.

There was no doubt that he gave us his best sales pitch, but a lot of what he said made good sense, particularly given our lack of understanding of the markets. As we drove home, we decided that we'd definitely put our investments into the hands of a professional. The big challenge was finding the right person. We still had a few more interviews to go.

As we pulled up in front of our house, it seemed perfectly appropriate that Hazen would be sitting on his front porch, perusing the day's paper.

I crossed the street to his yard. "We've just taken the plunge, Hazen."

He lowered his newspaper. "Being a boomer, that could mean many things. Could you qualify that statement?"

"The financial plunge. We interviewed a prospective financial adviser this afternoon," Pieter said, coming up behind me.

"Yikes. You two sound serious about this financial plan. That means I'd better finish up the Hazen Armstrong lecture series. We still have to talk about mutual funds. Say, what do you have on tonight?"

"Absolutely nothing," I replied.

"Great. It feels like summer this evening. Let's barbecue—the great American rite of passage into summer. In fact, I just picked up some ready-made burgers from Bread and Circus over on Washington Street. You have to thank the boomers for bringing convenience foods and gourmet items together into partnership—saving time while eating healthy. You two go get the kids. I saw Malcolm bring Emily home from school this afternoon, so I know they're in there," he said.

"Yeah, but who knows what state the house is in . . . ," I replied. "Actually, a barbecue sounds great, but let me raid my fridge and bring over the salad stuff. Is it a deal?"

"Deal," replied Hazen. "Now let's get going. We have a lot to cover tonight."

———

"Come around the back," said Hazen, spying us crossing the street with the kids in tow. "The grill is on and ready."

"You must have a demographic stat on barbecuing," said Pieter. "It's quick and easy—the boomers love it."

"I'm sure I could find one for you, Pieter, but I have something for you that's even better than a statistic."

I laughed. "What could that be, Hazen? You eat and breathe numbers."

"You obviously haven't tried these burgers," he proclaimed as we followed him along the path leading into his backyard.

Hazen found croquet mallets for the kids; wickets were already set up on his lawn. Armed with gigantic wooden hammers, the kids went off to do battle with one another. I positioned myself so that I could keep an eye on the action. I didn't want the genteel pastime of croquet to deteriorate into a contact sport.

"Well, it looks as if we're ready for our last installment," said Hazen, joining Pieter and me on the patio. "Mutual funds, the ultimate boomer investment. In the 1990s, mutual funds have grown fivefold. Now, let me spend a moment telling you what a mutual fund is. A mutual fund is a pool of capital (cash) that has been put together for a common, or mutual, purpose. The capital comes from investors—people like you. The pool of cash is managed by a professional manager who carries out the mandate of the fund under strict guidelines. Funds put out something called a simplified prospectus, which details operating costs, fees, the objectives of the fund, and other relevant information. Kind of dry stuff, most times, but important reading nevertheless. The investor is actually the owner of the fund and should have a full understanding of the specific goals and objectives of the fund. The cash in mutual funds is invested in different types of assets, including stocks, bonds, mortgages, and money market securities. The type of investment selected reflects the mandate of the fund. Now, obviously, you can't know everything. This is where your adviser's role is critical."

"Yes, the fellow we met with this afternoon was talking about the difficulty faced by an individual when looking at past-performance stats of a mutual fund," I said.

"That's a good example of what I'm talking about. Ideally, you'll end up with an adviser knowledgeable about who is managing the fund you're interested in and what the future plans are for that fund—information you'd be hard-pressed to discover on your own," Hazen replied.

"It sounds confusing," I said, shaking my head.

"Keep this simple fact in mind, then," Hazen replied. "In the end, funds can be classified into two basic areas: growth or income funds. An income fund invests in things like bonds and money market instruments, providing its owner with current income. A growth fund, on the other hand, holds equities—stocks. At this stage in your investing career, you'll probably want to concentrate on growth funds. And it's advisable, if you've got a few thousand dollars to invest, to spread your money into different funds in order to spread your exposure. Even stock funds can be broken down. You've probably heard about large-, mid-, and small-cap funds. The 'cap' refers to market capitalization of a company, which is calculated by multiplying the number of shares outstanding by the price of those shares. So, a small-cap fund would invest primarily in companies with relatively smaller capitalizations—smaller companies. Given the amount of money the boomers will be handing over to institutions over the next twenty years, I'd recommend keeping an eye on large-cap funds. Funds can be broken down even further into industries. You can find gold funds or funds with a geographic focus, such as Asian or European funds. But an adviser is the best person to help you with all these details. I'm going to focus my remarks tonight on equity mutual funds because, as you now know, your generation is headed straight for the stock market."

"After our discussion today with the stockbroker, I'm feeling slightly overwhelmed," I admitted. "There's so much we need to learn about the markets—all those companies, all those stock listings, everything changing day-to-day. How can we possibly keep track of everything?"

"That's where mutual funds come in. They can simplify the way you invest in the stock market. But even the mutual fund market is becoming complicated with all the different types of funds around. Let me give you some local examples to think about," Hazen said, passing us some photocopied sheets. "This is just a taste of the variety of choices—there's huge diversity. Now, the first is called the Eaton Vance Income Fund of Boston. To invest in this fund, you have to be comfortable with a fair bit of risk. This aggressive fund invests in bonds of the high-yield, high-risk variety. Compare this to one of the granddaddies of funds: Fidelity Magellan Fund. Its portfolio is predominantly made up of common stocks. It's very large, a stable fund that has performed extremely well over the past number of years. Third, let's take a look at Scudder Capital Growth Fund. Like the Fidelity fund, this fund also invests primarily in stocks, but focuses its emphasis on relatively new companies. The interesting thing about this Scudder fund is the fact that it's a no-load fund—you don't pay fees when you buy it or sell it. That means that a financial adviser won't buy this one for you—this is a fund you'll be buying on your own. Lastly, I've included another large Boston fund: Putnam Vista Fund. Putnam tends to charge higher fees than many fund companies—here, see the maximum front-end sales charge is 5.75 percent," said Hazen, pointing to the bottom of the sheet containing the Putnam information.

"But, look up here," he continued, pointing to a chart showing the fund's growth. "This fund has posted very strong numbers in recent years. I've shown you these four funds to point out the variety out there. It's tough to track all the different options. That's why I'm recommending professional advice. Look, you've already received a pile of information from the broker. The best way to get a feel for this stuff is to read through the material. Any questions? Your adviser will be able to answer them. The key, of course, is finding an adviser who gives answers you can trust. That's why it's smart to deal with advisers your friends have already dealt with—somebody who has a proven track record, whom you can count on. Mutual funds also allow you to access the stock market with small amounts of money. If you buy individual stocks through a full-service brokerage, a minimum of $100 in fees could apply for each transaction. Now a discount broker could charge half of that, but if you are committing $500 each month to your savings, either of those costs are way out of line, seriously cutting into any profits you'll ever make on your investments."

"Funny you should have pulled the amount of $500 out of the air," Pieter said. "That's exactly the amount we were planning on investing each month. We've decided we're going to deposit Meredith's salary straight into our IRA accounts."

"Well, my suggestion would be to discuss the costs and fees with your adviser, but don't get too caught up with front-load, no-load, and back-end-load funds. You know what I'm talking about when I speak about loads?" Hazen asked.

"I'm pretty sure—you were talking about loads when you gave us the examples of the four Boston funds, but I wouldn't mind a refresher," I replied.

"Okay. A load is what the industry calls a commission or sales charge. Front-end-load funds charge commission at the time the fund is purchased. Neither no-load nor back-end-load funds charge a commission at the time of purchase. No-load fund—well, that's self-explanatory. In a back-end-load fund, the sales charge is deducted when you sell. This is the sort of detailed information you'll need to discuss with your adviser. The key concepts to remember are suitability of the fund for your portfolio and the fund's performance. Keep in mind that the most important elements are to get in early and give your investments plenty of years to compound. Two other things to think about—rates of return and asset allocation. Now let me do a quick calculation. You're both about forty, so $500 each month at, let's say, 12 percent will work out to be approximately $950,000 if you retire at sixty-five."

"Do you think we can get 12 percent on our investments?" I asked.

"With a boom coming at the market, I'd say you can," Hazen replied. "Mutual funds are perfect for your generation. They're time-friendly and user-friendly—a great combination for busy boomers. They allow you to be in the market with an educated guide. Think of it this way. If you were lost and someone handed you a map, would you use it?"

"Of course," answered Pieter. "But I don't see what geography has to do with the stock market."

"Think of the stock market as a foreign country. The professional managers who are responsible for mutual funds are the maps to that country, guiding you through the stock market. Whether you use a map to head into that unknown territory is up to you. In other words, you can invest in the stock market directly or, using a map, go into the markets through mutual funds. But just like maps, there's great variety in the way managers tend their respective funds. For example, some managers are more aggressive than others, some more conservative. This is where you seek your adviser's advice. He or she will be able to tell you who's who when it comes to fund managers."

"The popularity of mutual funds is no real demographic surprise, is it?" said Pieter. "The boomers are heading into their prime saving years, and mutual funds are a pretty easy place to invest."

"Exactly," replied Hazen. "The boomers are showing up like clockwork in the mutual fund market. Perfectly predictable. It's actually quite amusing. Your generation fancies itself to be individualistic, but in the end you tend to head at the same thing at the same time. A mutual approach." Hazen chuckled at his pun and went to fuss with the barbecue.

"But there's more to this than boomers buying mutual funds," he said. "Think about what I've told you. Most of the mutual funds are being purchased via retirement accounts. Remember what I told you about interest rates?"

We nodded. "They're going to stay low for years," I said.

"Right," Hazen continued, closing the lid on the grill and returning to his seat. "Listen to these stats. First, the entire New York Stock Exchange—the premiere market— is $8 trillion in size. That's a fraction of the size of the real estate market across this country. Now look what's poised to hit the NYSE. The amount invested in the mutual fund industry currently stands at about $4 trillion. Roughly $2 trillion of that is invested in stocks at this time. Fully $2 trillion is in a variety of income funds, and you know what interest rates are likely to do. So, I'd suggest we'll see a significant portion of that money move into growth funds. Now, here's something else to add into the mix—the pension industry. The pension industry in this country is well over $6 trillion. Remember, these institutions are funded by boomers with increasing amounts of money to put away for retirement.

"Here's another detail: the bond market also totals trillions of dollars. How much of that will leak into equities as rates decline and stay low? Here's the last stat to chew on. Look at what we have stashed away in commercial banks. It amounts to over $3 trillion. Let's face it, there are plenty of people who, no matter what, will continue keeping their money in a good solid bank. But guess what? The banks sell mutual funds too. I'd suggest that plenty of boomers who would never consider entering the stock market directly will enter it quite happily—indirectly—by buying an equity mutual fund at the bank. I think we'll see a large portion of their deposits moving over to the mutual funds side of the banking ledger. So, what's the reason for all these stats?"

I laughed. "To confuse us."

Hazen continued, unfazed. "I'm trying to show you the power of the boom and the fact that its power is building. It's going to hit the stock market in a wide variety of ways, ways that didn't exist until recently. All those institutions will be competing for a scarce resource, bidding up the price as a result. Now, I think our burgers are done to a turn," said Hazen, taking another look at his barbecue. "Why don't we call the kids in from their croquet match? I have just a couple of other points to make about funds, then we can tuck into our dinner."

The kids came running when called, mallets in hand. There's something about those first few barbecues of the season. Everything smells and tastes so good—especially when somebody else is doing the cooking. As we carried our things indoors, Hazen continued his lecture.

"Let me tell you why I believe stocks, in general, and equity mutual funds, specifically, will be the ultimate boomer commodity. I'd suggest that the markets will be hit much harder by the boom than was the real estate market. Not only do we have to consider the issue of supply and demand, but we also have to keep in mind that stocks are a commodity that are both hoarded and accumulated," said Hazen. He turned to the children and asked them to set the table for dinner. Once again, they cheerfully complied. Much more fun to set the table at someone else's house.

"What do you mean, hoarded and accumulated?" I asked.

"Think about it. When the boom hit the school system, an enormous pressure was placed on it. But the boom moved pretty quickly through the system. You spent only one year in second grade before moving on to third grade," Hazen explained.

"Not necessarily. Second grade was the toughest three years of Meredith's life," Pieter joked. The kids overheard that one, returning from the dining room all grins. I scooted them away, telling them their dad was just trying to be funny.

"Many commodities are hit by the boom but not held long term, not hoarded," Hazen continued. "Some commodities have been hoarded by the boomers but not accumulated. Real estate is a good example of that. Generally, people stay in their homes for a while—they hoard them, but they don't usually accumulate them. Most people have one home at a time and maybe a cottage, like you two. But think about the mutual fund market and the pressure exerted on stocks. You don't sell last year's investment to buy new mutual funds. No, not only do you hoard mutual funds, you also keep accumulating as much as you can, for as long as you can. We keep accumulating for years to build up enough reserves to fund our retirement. That's how this commodity differs from the others the boom has already hit. And that's what gives this commodity such tremendous upside potential—boomers want and need as much of it as they can lay their hands on. Put this in perspective: the average boomer has roughly twenty-five years to go before retirement. Boomers have only really been pressuring the market for less than five years and have already demonstrated their powerful muscle. Think what they could do over the next twenty years."

"But, Hazen, we hear so much about early retirement these days," I stated while he sliced a loaf of French bread. "Ruth and I are hearing about considerable job dissatisfaction amongst boomers. Plenty of them might want to leave the work force early. Won't that trend have an effect on the markets?"

"I wonder how that trend will play out in the future," he said. "Previous generations indicated that they wanted to retire early—until they hit retirement age. Then things changed and they started to think about working longer. In the last forty years, the average retirement age has crept down to sixty-three. Now keep in mind that the boom is partly responsible for that downward trend. Not only did the boom push out those ahead of it into early retirement, but it also gave that earlier generation the wherewithal to retire early. Remember, your parents' generation profited from the boom and could afford to retire early. Boomers may not be so lucky. Plus, small Generation X isn't going to physically push the older boomers to retire. If workers' jobs aren't lost with the introduction of new technology, industry probably isn't going to be in any hurry to see you leave either. Older workers tend to be more productive, therefore more valuable. Surprise! See, old guys have some use—besides serving up dinner." Hazen gave the salad a quick toss.

"Before we head into the dining room, there's one more issue I want to raise. It's how the boomers hit a market. If you think about it, the process is always the same. The boomers need quantity first and quality second. Take cars, for instance. Do you remember what a Toyota looked like when it first hit North American markets? They were small and cheap and they sold like hotcakes because boomers were in the quantity years for cars. Well, you all got older, and see what a Toyota looks like today? It's called a Lexus, and it certainly isn't cheap. Toyota is a smart company. They've moved with the boomers into the quality-car years. It took American car makers a number of years to figure out this demographic shift. Cars provide one example of this quantity-to-quality phenomenon. It repeats itself over and over again in virtually every market the boomers hit. Look at clothing, housing, home furnishings.

"What does this mean for the stock market? Right now, boomers are buying quantity. Look at the recent jump in mutual fund sales. Boomers will move into quality years, but as I mentioned earlier, they'll hold on to their quantity. Unlike a car, they won't trade it in. But what will quality look like in the mutual fund market? I predict we'll be seeing funds built like individual portfolios and niche mutual funds. If you're into environmental issues, there will be plenty of environmental funds to choose from. Similarly, there will be more funds that target extremely narrow investments—emerging markets in Eastern Europe, for example, or the gold industry, let's say. In the meantime, however, quantity is still key for boomers and mutual funds. Okay, let's head for the table," Hazen exclaimed, leading us into the dining room.

The kids had done a perfect job of setting the table. I made a mental note to remind them of their abilities when we returned home to our own dining room.

As we took our seats, Hazen said, "There's just one more thing before I forget—we old guys get forgetful sometimes, you know," he laughed. "The mutual fund industry looks very attractive for years to come. But that doesn't necessarily mean you have to buy funds. You may want to talk to your adviser about buying stocks of the companies that manage mutual funds, including mutual fund companies and banks. Remember we discussed boomer stocks? Well, companies that sell mutual funds are the ultimate boomer stock. The mutual fund industry is where it's at for the boomers now and in the foreseeable future. Franklin Templeton is a good example of the type of mutual fund company you might invest in. It recently received a five-star rating from *Worth* magazine and—best of all—it trades publicly. There's a great saying about the stock market asserting that it's made up of three components: interest rates, earnings, and psychology. Well, it's time to add a fourth component: demographics. Now, before we start dinner, I have a gift for my favorite pupils to thank you for looking after my house," Hazen said, handing me a prettily wrapped object that looked suspiciously like a book.

"It's this year's *Morningstar Mutual Fund 500*," Hazen said as I tore into the paper. "It's the ultimate guide of the 500 most promising funds to help you and your adviser figure out what you need."

With that, Hazen began serving his specialty. We had to acknowledge that, in addition to knowing a fair bit about the boom, he was also a pretty good cook. We arranged that he'd be responsible for our Friday-night dinner at the cottage.

16

Life . . . Aha!

Equilibrium and disequilibrium. Hazen liked to talk about commodities moving in and out of equilibrium and disequilibrium. We'd heard about the school system, the real estate market, interest rates, and, now, the stock market. As I packed for our cottage weekend, I had the distinct feeling that our family had spent the past year moving from an unsettled period of disequilibrium to a satisfying plateau of equilibrium. And the cottage, together with the people who would be there with us this weekend, was a critical part of that good, stable feeling.

During the past couple of years, the cottage had taken a backseat in our lives. Worried about finances, busy with job changes, juggling the kids' lives along with our own, for us the cottage had become almost a burden. I'd argued that we should sell it. But Spofford Lake just wouldn't let Pieter go. He had spent his childhood summers there, and it's still the place he needs to go when his batteries require a boost. Upon reflection, I could see all of us needed the place; we were all better after some downtime at the cottage. As part of our life plan, Pieter and I made a commitment to one another: we'd spend more time at the cottage from here on in. This weekend launched the fulfillment of that promise.

During the week leading up to our departure, there had been numerous trips to Hank's for everything, including a new kitchen sink. Pieter planned on replacing the old leaky antique that we'd used for decades. Pieter the Plumber, the kids called him, knowing full well that all his plumbing skills were theoretical, acquired straight out of a book he'd picked up at somebody's garage sale. Just in case (not that I didn't trust Pieter's plumbing skills), I also bought a big bucket from Hank. It would serve nicely if, by some weird chance, we didn't have a kitchen sink for a spell.

Later Friday afternoon, I was loading duffle bags into the back of the van and Pieter was strapping the sink to its top as Ruth pulled up.

"What! Are you telling me there's no plumbing at this place?" she cried as she got out of her car. She and Hazen planned to drive up together—our van was full to bursting with food, clothes, toys, and books—plenty of books. Reading was a DeMarco family passion at the cottage.

"What's the matter, Ruth? Don't like roughing it?" Pieter shouted from his perch atop the van.

"Ha! One fool can tell another, as my uncle used to say. You're pulling my leg, Pete. Meredith told me you were going to plumb this summer. I know you've got running water up there," she said. I could tell we were in for a weekend of witty repartee.

"Ruth, can you come help me load this van? I don't have a clue how I'm going to fit all this in," I said, gesturing to a front lawn full of bags, boxes, and assorted cottage stuff.

"I have the answer. Hazen and I will take the kids. That should free up some space," Ruth said, waving to Hazen, who was crossing the street loaded with bags of groceries. Many hands make light work, and in less than three hours we were pulling up the lane to the cottage.

One of my favorite cottage moments is the arrival. It's the smell of the air. Stepping from the car, I'm always nearly bowled over by the scent of the place—the sweetness of pine, the muskiness of the dirt, the freshness of the air sweeping in from the lake. A few deep breaths and the cares of the city vanish—for the weekend, at least. As Hazen, Ruth, and the kids got out of the car, I watched Ruth taking the time to breathe in the place, just like me. " 'In all things of nature there is something of the marvelous,' " she said to no one in particular.

"Your uncle, right?" Pieter said, untying the sink.

"Actually, no. Somebody a little older than him. Aristotle," she laughed.

"So this is your little piece of heaven," Hazen said to Pieter. "Very nice. You know, I always meant to buy a cottage, but I somehow never got around to it."

We all laughed. "Come on, Hazen. You always get around to everything you really want to do in life," I said.

"Well, actually, what I really want to do right now is take a peek around your cottage and then head out to the deck and watch the sun set," Hazen replied.

"Sounds like a great plan. Mind if we all join you?" said Pieter, handing boxes and bags to whomever was standing empty-handed. We unlocked the cottage and discovered—to our pleasure—that the place was in great shape. Our only immediate tasks were to open the windows and disarm the mousetraps. The kids headed out to explore the place.

"Before we go out to the deck, why don't we sort out the sleeping arrangements and move all of this luggage out of the living room," Pieter suggested, picking up Ruth's bag. "We don't have a lot of extra space up here. We always seem to end up one bedroom shy when we have guests. Ruth, how about you taking the extra bedroom? Hazen, the pull-out couch isn't too uncomfortable. Sorry we're not better equipped."

"Don't worry, I'll be fine in here with Ruth," said Hazen, taking her bag from Pieter. Pieter turned to me and we had one of our eye conversations. Ruth caught the exchange.

"Hey, come on, you two, don't be such prudes," said Ruth. "If we can have a child together, I think we can share a bed at a cottage. You boomers are all the same. You talk a good game, but at heart you're as old-fashioned as they come."

"Child?" I said. "You mean that Hazen is Dylan's father?"

Ruth turned to Hazen. "Didn't you tell them?"

"I thought you must have," he replied, shrugging his shoulders. "I just assumed they knew."

For an instant the four of us stared at one another, then Ruth launched into her deep chuckle.

"Marriage just wasn't for us," she began. "You've known both of us long enough to realize we're both pretty independent types. Although we lived separately, we raised Dylan together. We never fit into the normal mold, but in the end everything was okay. You run your life the way you need to run your life. The trick is realizing what it is you truly need. Although both of us were completely committed to Dylan, Hazen and I valued our independence."

Hazen nodded. "It's such a common boomer trait," he said. "Boomers like to think they invented the alternative life-style."

"Well," I said, "now I understand the significance of your photos of the three of you, Hazen. This is starting out to be an interesting weekend. And I think I could use a little quiet time on the deck. Would anyone like to join me?"

The reaction was unanimous and we set off, hauling our old wooden Adirondack chairs out from under the deck and giving them a quick brush-off, removing the winter's debris and an intricate network of spider webs. Soon the four of us were comfortably settled. I could see Emily and Malcolm through the trees, standing by the edge of the lake, tossing stones into the water. As long as they weren't throwing them at each other, everything in this world was perfect.

Hazen broke the contented silence. "You know, this cottage is a terrific symbol for your generation. Actually, you two are still a bit young for this thing. The cottage mentality, as I call it, usually kicks in around the mid- to late-forties. The front edge of the boomers has just arrived there. The full force of the younger generation will be there later this decade."

"And what is the cottage mentality?" Pieter asked.

Hazen sat gazing at the lake for a moment. "Your generation has been going full speed for the past twenty years, seeing what it could shake out of this old world. I think you're going to see a shift in behavior as the boomers hit solid middle age. It's like we were discussing at our last lecture. They've realized that life is not a quantity game; it's all about quality. This insight is the result of aging—and we're watching a large group of boomers hit the process all at once. Think about it. In the past, a weekend away might have been a fast-paced scene with lots of activity and action. Now, a quiet weekend on a lake with a few friends and family is the ideal. Cottages are a big part of that. I think your group is looking for ways to slow it down but, in keeping with the boomer mentality, continue to enjoy yourselves."

"That's consistent with my opinions," responded Ruth, sounding positively professorial. "If boomers can afford it, they're going to treat themselves very well."

We lapsed into silence once again, hearing only the kids' chatter floating up from the water's edge. I realized that this was the first time we'd spent with Hazen and Ruth together. Our two Buddhas were finally talking to us at the same time.

"We're watching society change gears once again," said Ruth. "It happens so dramatically when there's one huge generation dictating the Zeitgeist of an era."

"Hold it right there," I piped up. "You're sounding like an academic. What does Zeitgeist mean?"

"It's actually a handy term for talking about you boomers. It refers to the intellectual, moral, and cultural climate of an era. And the boomers have hijacked the agenda ever since they arrived on this planet. Look at the 1960s: sex, drugs, and rock 'n' roll. Who do you think were the brains behind that decade? It certainly wasn't your parents. But as one of the most famous products of the '60s went on to say: 'I just had to let it go.'"

"I thought you only quoted Aristotle," Pieter quipped.

"Nope. Every once in a while I quote John Lennon. Boomers have this amazing ability to think of themselves as much younger than they in fact are. I bet you're shocked when store clerks call you ma'am, right, Meredith?"

"You're darn right. I always look around to see if there's an old lady standing behind me."

"You all perceive yourselves to be younger than your chronological ages, but in fact boomers are starting to slow down, step into the next phase of life. This progression is going to show up in all sorts of places—our savings patterns, the way we spend our time, the way we look at our careers. Look at how it's affecting public policy, this push for safer, family-oriented communities. Cottages are a part of that. Let's face it. You folks aren't kids any more."

"But you will continue to have your usual large impact on the world," said Hazen. "From an investment perspective, I predict that we'll see cottages pan out to be a great investment."

Ruth said, "It's not just money, Hazen. It'll be a good life investment too. There's lots to be said for slowing down a bit and evaluating where you are in life."

We chatted until nightfall wrapped us in darkness. The kids wandered up and started to raid the coolers for snacks.

"Hey, bring some of that stuff out here," I shouted. The two of them dragged an entire cooler out to the deck.

I laughed. "You characters have a bit to learn about food presentation."

"Aw, Mom, we're at the cottage, if you didn't notice," Malcolm retorted.

"Exactly," said Hazen, rummaging around to see what the cooler would yield. He extracted a handful of carrot sticks and turned to Pieter. "Let me change the topic completely. Where are you and your associates at with BoomerBytes?"

"I'm glad you asked," Pieter replied. "I've been wanting to give you an update, just to hear your comments. I think I've learned my boomer lessons well. As you know, the Internet is taking off. And, as you are also aware, the boom is short of one key commodity: time. This generation displays some interesting traits. Boomers are the best-educated generation yet. They have an insatiable hunger for knowledge. Plus, as we've discussed, they like quality and are discerning customers. They don't mind paying a premium, but they want value for their money. They want convenience. They're into self-improvement. And a quick look around this dog-eat-dog job environment has taught them that they need to upgrade their skills constantly."

Pieter watched as Ruth and Hazen nodded their heads in unison. He continued: "So here's the idea. Why not let boomers sample a small taste of the work of many scholars, educators, and commentators—heck, any expert, for that matter—on a wide variety of topics? Using the

Internet, we can expose the latest, newest ideas to the boomers. BoomerBytes puts a sample of the work of these experts on our home page. It's a teaser. If the boomers like what they see, they contact us directly for additional information—it could be a book, an article, a tape, a CD, whatever. BoomerBytes is funded by the experts who want to see their material displayed there. Their material is put on the Net at no charge to them, and if their wares sell, we split the revenue. The more people surf the Net, the more stuff gets sold. Remember, you said the key is asking the right questions. Well, we're counting on people to be asking questions, and BoomerBytes will be a part of the solution."

"I like it," replied Hazen. "You've hit two key elements of the market. First, you're marketing directly to boomers. Like I've already told you, companies that offer something boomers want or need are poised for success. Who knows, you could become the Gerber of the 1990s. Second, you're in the right venue—the Net. Heck, even my favorite market is on its way to hitting the Net. There have already been plenty of examples of electronic stock trading on the Internet."

"I guess that only makes sense," said Ruth. "Combine technology and a desire for stocks and what do you get?"

"Well, first you should get cautious," answered Hazen. "You're not the only ones who know that the boomers are poised to hit the stock market. Like any booming market, the stock market will attract its fair share of unscrupulous characters trying to sell their wares. Arm yourself with knowledge and remember my two caveats: buy quality and think long term."

Just then I caught a glimpse of the first star on the horizon. "Look! Star light, star bright, what do we wish for tonight?"

"What about dinner?" Pieter said.

"What did you and Hazen prepare?" I inquired.

"Pasta and salad, " Hazen replied.

After dinner, the six of us sat at the table chatting about important and not-so-important stuff. At about 10:30, the kids wandered off to bed. And we moved onto a very serious cottage topic, books, reviewing what each of us had packed for the weekend.

"I'm in the middle of a collection of essays by Barbara Ehrenreich called *The Snarling Citizen*," Ruth informed us. "It captures the current Zeitgeist, doesn't it?"

"It's certainly what our work has been about," I answered. "The grumpiness of middle age."

"Actually, plenty of her essays are about aging and the boomers. She argues that boomers are poised to transform the way we think of death."

"Hey, that sounds like upbeat cottage reading," said Pieter. "Meredith, did you bring that brick I picked up for you at the library?"

"I did. And you'd better watch it, Pieter, or I'll drop it on your toe," I replied. "I brought along *God in All Worlds*. It's an anthology edited by Lucinda Vardey. The more discussions I've had with Ruth, the more I've realized that I have huge gaps in my spiritual knowledge. I guess I'm at a stage where I'm asking myself what it's all about."

"You're not alone," Hazen said. "As boomers have hit middle age, there's been a marked surge in interest about spirituality. Look at this New Age craze."

"What did you bring along?" I asked.

"I'm finishing up a book I reread every couple of years, *Great Expectations*."

"I'm impressed. You reread Dickens?" I asked.

"No, no, no. This *Great Expectations* is subtitled *America and the Baby Boom Generation*. It's by Landon Y. Jones and it's my boomer bible. It's a factual account of the boomers' progress through North American society. It contains great examples of the power of the boom. Let me tell you one. In January 1952, General Electric decided to make a big deal of their 75th anniversary. They offered to give every employee who had a child on October fifteenth of that year—the anniversary of the company's founding—five shares of General Electric. By announcing the offer in January, they gave all their employees a fair chance. At that time, G.E. had 226,000 employees. The G.E. bean counters figured there would be approximately thirteen births that day which they'd have to reward with a gift of shares. In fact, the G.E. employees produced 189 bundles of joy on October 15, 1952. Oops! And here's something just as amazing. If those children had held on to those shares till now, they'd be stting on over $30,000 worth of shares. The power of the stock market!"

"That's an interesting anecdote," Ruth responded. "Just another indicator of why we shouldn't underestimate what happens when the boom strikes. They're going to be every bit as potent and noticeable when they hit midlife."

"Here's another anecdote you might like," Hazen continued. "It all started back in 1946. That's when Dr. Benjamin Spock published a book entitled *The Common Sense Book of Baby and Child Care*. That book sold close to a million copies a year for the next twenty years. I guess I don't have to tell you why it was so popular."

"Dr. Spock's book revolutionized the way we raise children," Ruth said. "I know I bought a copy when Dylan was born."

Hazen smiled. "So did I."

"Pieter, what are you reading?" Ruth asked.

"As part of my BoomerBytes research, I picked up two books. *Age Wave: The Challenges and Opportunities of an Aging America* by Ken Dychtwald and Joe Flower, and *The Great Boom Ahead* by Harry Dent, Jr. I've heard what Hazen has to say about the power of the boom, now I'd like to know what others experts think. You know, it dawns on me as we sit here chatting that you should put your ideas on BoomerBytes, Dr. Armstrong and Dr. Schneider. Meredith and I have benefitted enormously from your financial and spiritual guidance. There must be plenty of other boomers like us who could learn from your wisdom."

"Hey, I've got it!" I said. "The Boom Doctors. You are our Boom Doctors, Hazen and Ruth."

"I don't know about that," replied Ruth, "but I hope we've taught you one thing—to think and ask questions. Like my uncle used to say, 'Ask advice from everyone, but keep your wits about you.'"

"Ruth's right. Or maybe I should say her uncle's right." Hazen chuckled. "We've given you some advice. What you do with it is up to you."

"I'm going to sleep on that one," said Pieter. "But before we go to bed, I want to propose a toast." He stood up and said, "You're right. It's our turn to run with the ball. To the Boom Doctors."

For Further Reading

Books

Beardstown Ladies Investment Club with Leslie Whitaker. *The Beardstown Ladies' Common-Sense Investment Guide*. New York: Hyperion, 1994.

Case, Samuel. *First Book of Investing: The Absolute Beginner's Guide to Building Wealth Safely*. Rocklin, CA: Prima Publishing, 1997.

Chilton, David. *The Wealthy Barber: Everyone's Common-Sense Guide to Becoming Financially Independent*, 3rd ed. Rocklin, CA: Prima Publishing, 1998.

Dent, Harry S., Jr. *The Great Boom Ahead: Your Comprehensive Guide to Personal and Business Profit in the New Era Prosperity*. New York: Hyperion, 1993.

————. *The Roaring 2000s: How to Achieve Personal and Financial Success in the Greatest Boom in History*. New York: Simon & Schuster, 1998.

Dychtwald, Ken and Flower, Joe. *Age Wave: The Challenges and Opportunities of an Aging America*. New York: Bantam Books, 1990.

Ehrenreich, Barbara. *The Snarling Citizen: Essays*. New York: HarperPerennial, HarperCollins Publishers, 1996.

Foot, David K. and Stoffman, Daniel. *Boom, Bust and Echo: How to Profit from the Coming Demographic Shift*. Toronto: Macfarlane Walter & Ross, 1996.

Jones, Landon Y. *Great Expectations: America and the Baby Boom Generation*. New York: Ballantine Books, 1981.

Kobliner, Beth. *Get a Financial Life: Personal Finance in Your Twenties and Thirties*. New York: Fireside, 1996.

Lynch, Peter and Rothchild, John. *Learn to Earn: A Beginner's Guide to the Basics of Investing and Business*. New York: Fireside, 1995.

Morningstar Mutual Fund 500, 1997-1998. Burr Ridge, IL: Irwin Professional Publishing, 1997.

Russell, Cheryl. *The Master Trend: How the Baby Boom Generation Is Remaking America.* New York: Plenum Press, 1993.

Thurow, Lester C. *The Future of Capitalism: How Today's Economic Forces Shape Tomorrow's World.* New York: Penguin Books, 1996.

Vardey, Lucinda. *God in All Worlds: An Anthology of Contemporary Spiritual Writing.* New York: Pantheon Books, 1995.

Yamada, Louise. *Market Magic: Riding the Greatest Bull Market of the Century.* New York: John Wiley & Sons, 1998.

Newsletters

The Boomer Report, Age Wave Communications Corporation, P.O. Box 608, Vandalia, OH 45377.

Software

Quicken Financial Planner, Intuit.

Magazines

American Demographics, P.O. Box 68, Ithaca, NY 14851

Fortune, P.O. Box 61490, Tampa, FL 33661-1490

Kiplinger's, Editors Park, MD 20782

Money, P.O. Box 60001, Tampa, FL 33660-0001

Worth, 575 Lexington Ave., New York, NY 10022

On the Web

AAII On-Line. http://www.aaii.org

Financenter. http://www.financenter.com

Money Online. http://www.money.com